The No-Worries Estate Planner

What you need to know for today, tomorrow, and the hereafter

Roy and Fran Bollinger

RLB/FAB Publishers
Simi Valley, California

First edition, 2021

Copyright © 2021 by **Roy and Fran Bollinger**

For permission requests, write to the publisher at the address below:

Roy and Fran Bollinger
4693 Hempstead Street
Simi Valley, CA 93063
rlbfab2@gmail.com

Although the publisher and authors have used reasonable care in preparing this book, the information it contains is distributed "as is" and without warranties of any kind. *No-Worries* is not intended as legal or financial advice, and not all the recommendations may be suitable for your situation. The information provided is from observation and research of how laws have been applied to situations and not intended as legal expertise. Laws change in an instant and may have been valid when the book was written but are no longer valid the day of book publishing. Even so, these laws are still relevant to our stories as seen through the eyes of a layman and not from legal or financial experts. Be diligent in doing your own factchecking. Professional legal and financial advisors must be consulted as needed. The book is meant to give you an easily read authors' interpretation on procedures you need to do and be aware of to protect yourself and your family. Neither the publisher nor the author shall be liable for any costs, expenses, or damages resulting from use of or reliance on the information contained in this book.

Ordering Information:

Special discounts are available on quantity purchases by corporations, associations, and others. For details, contact the publisher at the address above.

Project Manager: Marla Markman, MarlaMarkman.com
Editor: Tammy Ditmore, Editmore.com
Cover and Book Design: Kelly Cleary, KellyMaureenCleary@gmail.com

ISBN: 978-1-7361612-0-3 (Softcover)
ISBN: 978-1-7361612-2-7 (eReaders)

Library of Congress Control Number: 2020922735

Names: Bollinger, Roy, author. | Bollinger, Fran, author.
Title: The no-worries estate planner : what you need to know for today , tomorrow , and the hereafter /
Roy and Fran Bollinger.
Description: Simi Valley, CA: RLB/FAB Publishers, 2021.
Identifiers: LCCN: 2020922735 | ISBN: 978-1-7361612-0-3 (pbk.) | 978-1-7361612-2-7 (ebook)
Subjects: LCSH Retirement--United States--Planning. | Retirement income--Planning. | Personal finance. | Estate planning--United States. | Wills--United States. | Tax planning--United States. | BISAC BUSINESS & ECONOMICS / Personal Finance / Money Management | BUSINESS & ECONOMICS / Personal Finance / Retirement Planning
Classification: LCC HG179 .B65 2021 | DDC 332.024/01--dc23

Printed in the United States of America

The No-Worries Estate Planner is dedicated to
our family and friends
who from the beginning have been unconditionally supportive.
We have valued all their input.

Roy and I are so fortunate to have raised three
talented and caring individuals,
Susan, Diane, and Roy Jr.

They, in turn, married talented and caring partners:
Gaylord, Todd, and Toni.

Their union has produced six loving,
smart grandchildren:
Nate, Brandon, Allison, Matthew, Royce, and Issy,
our cheering section.

Table of Contents

INTRODUCTION
What's Inside
1

Roy and I are ecstatic about sharing our workbook. We have helped many family and friends, and we know firsthand what works and what doesn't. This information is shared with you as not legal advice but friendly observations. Our workbook is different from the many traditional estate planning and organization books. We not only provide forms to complete but also add the knowledge of why these forms are important to you. We give voice to the people who have shared their experiences with us. We share their stories so their misunderstandings and interpretation of laws do not become yours.

CHAPTER 1
Alzheimer's Disease: A Personal Story
5

More than 5 million Americans are living with Alzheimer's disease, and that number is climbing dramatically. Alzheimer and other dementias can wreak havoc in a family, especially if estate planning has not been done properly. In this chapter, we describe our family's experience with Alzheimer's and explain how it helped inspire us to create this workbook.

CHAPTER 2
Write It Down!
13

Do you know your doctor's name and phone number? Where do you store the papers you will need to file your taxes this year? Where do you keep your insurance policies? More important, would someone else be able to find this important information? This chapter gives you a place to bring together all your most important information so you—or a loved one—can easily locate it in an emergency.

CHAPTER 3
Passwords, User Names, Security Questions, Subscriptions, and Subscription Services
63

It's not enough anymore to know where to find your important papers because these days so much information is stored in your computer or in an online account. To access that digital information, you will probably need to remember multiple user names and dreaded passwords. This chapter will give you tips for simplifying your digital life while keeping your information safe and secure.

CHAPTER 4
Staying on Top of Bills and Payments
71

It can be tough to stay on top of your bills and keep track of payments for insurance, taxes, and other expenses that crop up. Set up a system for your household finances using the worksheets and other tips you find in this chapter. Creating a household finance system will make life easier whether you are a young parent caring for small children or an adult child trying to ensure your aging parents can continue to live independently. The worksheets in this chapter will make it easy to see what bills need to be paid and when.

CHAPTER 5
The Taxing Questions of Homeownership
81

Homeownership has many advantages, but there are downsides too. What happens if you inherit a home from Mom or Dad? Should you sell or keep it? Do you know how Proposition 13 will affect you? Check out this chapter before you make any decisions.

CHAPTER 6
Navigating the Retirement Account Labyrinth
89

Retirement accounts sound so simple. Put money in while you're working; take money out when you retire. Right? Wrong. Replace simple with complicated and confusing. These plans have been designed by financial experts, and users must follow a maze of government rules and regulations to stay out of trouble. This chapter will help you understand the differences between tax-deferred accounts, avoid the pitfalls of required minimum withdrawals, and walk you through the perils that come when you inherit an account.

CHAPTER 7
The Medicare, Medigap Maze
111

Medicare Part A, Part B, Part C, Part D. Medigap. Medicare Advantage. So many plans to choose from; so many questions; so much confusing language. Penalties for late enrollment. Caveats everywhere. Check out this chapter for help finding your way through the Medicare maze.

CHAPTER 8
End-of-Life Options
133

Many people will need long-term residential care for themselves or their loved ones. This chapter will examine some options, such as skilled-nursing and board and care facilities, palliative care, and hospice help. And it will give you a peek into what some of those options might cost you while explaining the End of Life Option Act.

CHAPTER 9
Funeral Planning
143

Times have changed, and families today have far more choices to make when a loved one dies. Cemetery or cremation? Burial in ground or a mausoleum? Ashes on the mantel, columbarium niche, scattered? Traditional funeral, military burial, memorial celebration? This chapter examines some of the options.

CHAPTER 10
Surviving Spouse Action Plan
179

So much to do. So many decisions that need to be made—NOW. Where is the information you need? Where should you start? We supply the worksheets and some step-by-step procedures to walk you through the process.

CHAPTER 11
Closing an Estate
221

Closing an estate is complicated, especially if you are an administrator, executor, or trustee. You may need professional help. But before you call in a lawyer, use the worksheets in this chapter to help you gather all the information you will need to accomplish all the tasks you can handle on your own. The more you do on your own, the less money you will pay the experts.

INTRODUCTION
What's Inside

This workbook has been created by Roy and Fran Bollinger, who wanted readers to have a friendly, easy-to-understand guide to help organize estate plans. They soon realized that making estate plans is not only for the future. It affects your life today, tomorrow, and in the hereafter. While the purpose of the guide is to share their life experiences to help you make informed decisions, they are not pretending to offer customized legal advice. Rather, they are offering you a better understanding of issues that influence your life. You will be better prepared if you decide to hire a lawyer or personal financial advisor.

The authors live in California, so the information presented in this book is based on California laws and statutes that may not apply in other states.

The decision to write this book was made after helping numerous relatives and friends work through their financial responsibilities while navigating the maze of illness and death. Some individuals had wills, while others relied on trusts. Some were dealing with a sudden death; others faced long illnesses. The authors encountered a variety of status situations: single, significant other, married, registered domestic partner, separated, divorced, and widowed. Each faced different questions and unique challenges.

Most people find trying to learn the ins and outs of insurance, elder care, funeral planning, wills, and estates overwhelming. This is especially true for anyone in the middle of a health crisis or dealing with a loved one's unexpected death. It's important to take the time to learn the basics and make a plan *before* a crisis.

This book will help you plan in advance for difficult days, so they won't be as complicated when they do arrive. Worksheets have been provided for many scenarios. Once you start completing the worksheets, you will find it becomes easier as you continue. You will receive satisfaction every time you complete a checklist or fill in a worksheet, knowing steps completed will be useful now and in the future. As you work your way through this book, you will be officially noting decisions and preferences so they can be legally recorded. You will no longer have to guess whether your loved ones know your thoughts.

Document, Document, Document

Estate planning involves far more than just creating a will or trust, although this is an absolutely necessary step for most people. But a will or trust will do your family members little good if they don't know where to find your important papers and possessions when needed. That's why it's so critical for you to get in the habit of documenting information *and* leaving a well-marked trail for your family.

No matter how much saving, planning, and implementing is done for an estate, it can become worthless if you accidentally miss a due date, break an IRS rule, or leave no information about where to find your important papers and valuables.

A person suffering with Alzheimer's disease may never realize he or she has a problem, and their loved ones may not recognize the gravity of that person's situation until the memory and reasoning abilities of the Alzheimer's patient have been severely impaired. By that time, it will be too late for a person suffering from Alzheimer's to help with needed decision-making or explain what estate planning has been put into place. At that point, relatives may become wistful and realize loved ones would have fared better if someone had taken the time to accumulate household information and created an action plan for what was needed to run the household. Written plans can sometimes help elders handle their affairs longer and live independently in their homes for a few extra years.

Hunting for Treasures

When a loved one dies or loses memory or other abilities due to Alzheimer's, accidents, or other problems, family members may face some unpleasant surprises if no one has been actively monitoring the estate planning. Not being able to find necessary paperwork, expensive heirlooms, or other "valuables" can be a nasty shock.

It is no coincidence riches are found in forgotten storage containers. In California, an auctioneer is allowed to sell the contents of a container to the highest bidder if storage rent has not been paid for a certain number of months. It is not unusual for people with Alzheimer's or other illnesses to forget to pay their bills—or even to forget that they have placed possessions in a storage container. The stars of the TV series *Storage Wars* often brag about profits of $20,000, $30,000, or even $60,000 made from one purchased container. How sad that some viewers watch and wonder, "Was that Dad's rare toy collection? The one we could never find when he died?"

One couple frequently bragged about the $25,000 in savings bonds they had stashed away, but their kids never knew any details or asked where the bonds were being stored. When their parents died, the kids never found a trace of the bonds. Had their parents cashed in the bonds and spent the money? Did someone steal the bonds? Were there ever any bonds in the first place? The kids never found out.

The California State Controller's Office stated in June 2018 that they held $9 billion in unclaimed cash and property. Each state is entitled to keep unclaimed money indefinitely and use the interest earned.

Another family knew that Mom and Dad owned a beach rental in Ventura. But they didn't know the taxes on the property were not being paid and were unaware it was being seized and sold to pay for back taxes. The situation could have been prevented if the family had been receiving more information.

Overcoming Excuses

There are lots of reasons people don't want to talk to their families or establish an estate plan.

- I'm embarrassed/ashamed to talk about sickness or death.
- I don't have time to worry about what happens in the future.
- I need to focus on my job right now.
- Not to worry; when I die the kids will know what to do.
- I don't have enough assets to be concerned.
- Things will work out, as always.

We've heard all these excuses, and unfortunately, we know they are so wrong. Many examples throughout this workbook demonstrate how and why things don't magically work without planning and action. All stories in the workbook are **true**. They have been included to help you see the pitfalls other individuals have fallen into—and help you understand how much information you are expected to know and share. Personal stories are easier to identify with than graphs and charts.

Talk It Over

We often have reservations about discussing finances with Mom and Dad. It is their money. They have worked a lifetime to accumulate savings. Why should we interfere?

We have seen far too many examples of how savings have been lost simply because individuals did not know about government rules, laws, and regulations. Or children have discovered too late their parents made devastating financial decisions or lost money to scammers when illness or dementia started to impair their reasoning abilities.

We encourage adult children and parents to work together to *each* complete a planner. In the process, the older generation can share valuable life experience and knowledge, while the younger generation can provide information on new ideas and updated laws. A packet of extra worksheets is available for purchase to accompany the planner.

Laws, ordinances, and statutes are confusing and complicated, and they change often. Don't take anything for granted. Always check facts. To verify how complicated estate planning is, we recommend you listen to Bill Handel's *Handel on the Law*, which can be heard as a podcast or on some radio stations. You will hear numerous callers seeking advice regarding estate blunders and the consequences they are facing.

Be aware that predators are successfully searching for a piece of your estate pie. They will not hesitate to grab unprotected money and possessions even if it means lying, cheating, or forcing people out of their homes and into the streets.

We don't want that to happen to anyone! That's why we've created this planner. So, turn the page and get going!

CHAPTER 1

Alzheimer's Disease
A Personal Story

Fran's mother, Frances Sax, gave proof to the theory of "survival of the fittest." She had made a cross-country move in an era when that was a difficult journey, raised two kids, been widowed twice, excelled at several jobs, enjoyed a variety of hobbies, and simply loved life. She worked hard to achieve the life of her dreams, but her family saw Alzheimer's take it all away.

Mom, Dad, Joe, and I arriving in the wild, wild, west. Elyria, Ohio, to Douglas, Arizona, 1,925 miles. Gas, 26 cents a gallon.

Road Trip to Arizona

Mom was always game for an adventure, so she didn't complain when Dad converted a school bus to carry the four of us—my parents, my brother Joe and me—from Ohio to Arizona in what might be called an early type of motor home. Dad's ingenuity meant we would not be crammed into a small vehicle for our long road trip, and we were able to carry all our possessions with us.

5

We did not have the conveniences of running water, conventional beds, toilet, shower, oven, or refrigerator. But Dad's converted bus was far ahead of its time, a prototype of future luxurious travel residences now seen on every thoroughfare.

Our excursion in 1948 predated most freeways and interstate highways. My dad, who had been a Navy photographer during World War II, loved drama and was in his element piloting his bus along narrow roads and winding mountain passes. My brother and I still have nightmares of him running cars off the road, our knuckles gleaming white as we hung onto the bars on the back of the seats, fearing for our lives.

Dad had learned there is safety in numbers, so he convinced his sister, Mary, and her husband, Russell, to purchase and convert their own school bus and travel with us. And that they did, with their two sons, Russ and David. Our bizarre caravan received many peculiar looks.

Tucson Veterans Hospital

Later, Mom and Dad divorced. I was married and living in California. Joe had been drafted into the army. Mom, always ambitious and hardworking, accepted employment at Tucson Veterans Hospital pushing a library/merchandise cart. Twenty-three years later, she retired as a secretary with lifetime medical and dental benefits and a small pension.

Retirement

After retiring, Mom was involved in a frenzy of activities, including bingo, bowling, church choir, women's club, and walking her beloved dog, Mitzie. One of her favorite activities was being a member of a dance club. She and Chuck, her handsome dance instructor, entered and won a variety of competitions, from square dancing to ballroom. She loved shopping and was on cloud nine when she found attire and jewelry to complement her dance routines. Mom believed we were not sent here for a long time but for a good time. She had fun and loved life.

Mom was eighty-six, living independently in Tucson, Arizona, when we received an alarming call from her friend Amy, who was concerned about Mom's mental state. Amy had arrived to pick up Mom for their weekly lunch and church bingo outing and was surprised to find her wearing funky pajamas, disheveled, with no memory of their outing.

Next, Mom's twin sister, Eleanor, informed us that Mom frequently drove long, confusing routes home from church activities. Mom was always ready for an escapade, but this was extreme even for her.

My brother, Joe, drove from his home in Scottsdale to Tucson to see for himself what was going on. He found a note from Mom's doctor advising her not to drive. Joe asked Mom about the note, and she snapped, "What are you talking about? There is nothing wrong with my driving."

Joe phoned me, so Roy and I drove from our home in Southern California to Tucson, where we all met with Mom's doctor. He informed us that he believed Mom was suffering from Alzheimer's disease. She should definitely not be driving or living alone.

The doctor promptly notified the DMV of his evaluation, and Mom's license was immediately revoked. But Mom continued to deny having a problem and insisted she would continue to drive. So, we disabled the car by disconnecting the battery cables.

California, Here We Come!

What to do? Mom was still independent enough to cook and clean for herself in her own home, but now she had no transportation to shop for food or socialize. We convinced her to come home with Roy and me to Simi Valley for a "short" visit. What none of us realized at the time was that she would never return to Tucson to live. It was a hard transition for all of us.

For months, Mom's focus would be to talk about going home to sing in the church choir or have lunch with a friend. Telephone book in hand, she would try to figure out how to get a cab and make a plane reservation. Not able to accomplish the task, she would reach for her purse. Whenever nervous or thinking of home, Mom would find comfort feeling her car and house keys we had left in her purse.

It was heartbreaking to watch her lose her memory while never losing her desire to return to Arizona and her old life. There was no way we could explain it was gone; Amy had

died of cancer; Beth was at a rehabilitation center recovering from a hip replacement; Rita had moved out of state. No friends, card games, dancing, or church socials were waiting for her—even if she were able to go home. Instead of trying to explain what was beyond her comprehension, we just kept persuading her to extend her visit for "a little longer."

Three Amigos to the Rescue

Roy, Joe, and Russ (Mom's superhero nephew) became known as the three amigos as they made multiple trips to Tucson to deal with all the details of our new reality. Their first trip was to sort paperwork and return with some of her personal items. Roy concentrated on retrieving tax and bank statements, insurance information, checks, utility bills, home title, and address book. Mom's car was sold to an appreciative relative.

For the next couple of years, the three amigos would meet in Tucson to repair Mom's beloved 1948 hacienda: roof, yard, plumbing. It took a while for all of us to realize that under no circumstance was there a chance Mom would be returning to her home. Unimaginable.

On one of the many repair trips, cigarette butts and beer bottles were found in and around the house. We hoped they had been left by an old flame who had come to visit because we did not want to face the likely reality that someone unknown had accessed her house. Worried this could lead to vandalism or worse, we made the hard decision to sell her home.

Because I was caring for Mom, I could not help with any of the chores involved in getting the house ready to sell. Relatives helped with the *gigantic* task of clearing the house of accumulated treasures and living memories of her many accomplishments. They filled tables and tables with merchandise for a neighborhood yard sale and made *many, many* trips to Goodwill, then finally rented multiple trash bins. Eventually, the house was cleared, cleaned, and sold. *Mission accomplished.* The proceeds from the yard and house sale were put into an account for Mom's care.

Bingo, Bingo, and More Bingo

Life remained relatively simple for the next couple of years. Mom continued to agree to stay with us for "just a little longer," but she never stopped wanting to go home, especially around her birthday because that was when she was accustomed to Joe's visit. He would take her out to a fancy restaurant for a birthday celebration.

Roy, already retired, took Mom to doctor and dentist appointments. He faithfully made sure she took her daily medicines and consistently used her eye drops. I was working as an office manager for Simi Valley Unified Schools, so Roy would often drive Mom to restaurants to meet me on my lunch hour. Saturdays I would take her to play bingo at the Thousand Oaks Senior Center. Every morning, she would wake up, sit down for coffee, and look at the newspaper to see if it was Saturday, our day to play. On the Saturdays I had other commitments and could not take her to bingo, we would leave a Friday paper on the table so she would not realize this was her day for a Saturday outing and be upset. Mom's golden rule: *never ever miss bingo or a chance to play a slot machine.*

Spiraling Down the Rabbit Hole

Life changed again when Mom twisted her ankle and had to go to the hospital and then rehabilitation. I expected her to freak out when the ambulance arrived after her accident, but she loved the attention of the handsome young paramedics. She had a big cat's grin when carried out of our house on a stretcher, waving like royalty.

Her happiness dissolved into confusion during her stay in the hospital and rehab facility. When I visited her, Mom would think I was her sister. She would look at me and ask, "Where is Fran? Why doesn't she come and see me? When can I go home?" My heart would break every time.

Because Mom now needed to be in a wheelchair, she couldn't return to our home. We could not lift her or give her all the care she needed. I had never wanted to place her in a care facility, but circumstances and her condition left us no other choice. My husband, always thinking ahead, had researched residential versus nursing home care.

Residential care is provided in a home that offers staff supervision twenty-four hours a day. Meals are provided and residents get help with their personal needs. Most residential care homes can take a maximum of six patients at one time; costs are typically lower than for skilled-nursing facilities.

Skilled-nursing facilities, commonly called nursing homes, provide the same services as residential care but can also provide more extensive healthcare. They have extended staff and at least one registered nurse on duty at all times. Costs for long-term care are higher in California than in the majority of states.

I've provided some details of the costs of Mom's care from 2004 through 2007 and also some examples of what that same care would have cost in 2019. I hope these charts will give you a better idea of what to expect if you must pay for long-term care.

Approximate Cost of Mom's Care, California, 2004–2007

Type of Care	Day	Month	Year
Six-person residential care home, two residents per room	$99.45	$3,025	$36,300
Skilled nursing, three residents per room	$180	$5,475	$65,700

Approximate Costs for Similar Care, California, 2019

Type of Care	Day	Month	Year
Six-person residential care home, one resident per room	$155	$4,714	$56,575
Skilled nursing, two residents per room	$255	$7,650	$93,075

New Living Arrangements

We transferred Mom to a six-person residential care home, where she shared a room with another patient. Much to my surprise, she loved it! What was the secret sauce? Pampering and attention, which she received in abundance.

The first Saturday I picked Mom up for lunch and bingo, I was anxious. After our outing, would she insist on coming home with me? How could I tell her that she had lost another home and would have to now live at this facility? When our day of fun was finished, I wheeled her up the sidewalk to the facility, still worried that she would object to staying here. Her caregiver opened the front door. Mom smiled and looked up at him, saying it was nice to see him again after such a long time. The caregiver quickly wheeled her into the house. She did not ask to come home with me. You never know!

We enjoyed smooth sailing for the next couple of years until Mom fell and broke her hip. She had successful hip replacement surgery, followed by rehabilitation, and a return to her residential care home. Unfortunately, she had developed bedsores in rehabilitation. She now required extensive care in skilled nursing and could no longer stay in residential living.

Another Move

She was transferred to a skilled-nursing home, and I lamented that Mom was again losing her familiar surroundings. In the nursing facility, she shared a room with two other ladies, and I was again reminded that sharing was good for her. Always social, Mom felt stimulated when there were people coming and going. For a while, I was able to take her to church services and her favorite Saturday bingo games. Although I knew she was well cared for in skilled nursing, I still hoped she would be able to return to her former, cozy residential home.

Complications

However, by the time Mom was well enough to return to residential living, we were reluctant to move her. If we moved her back to her preference, residential living, and she needed to return to skilled nursing, her chances of returning to her current skilled-nursing home were slim to nonexistent. Her current skilled-nursing home was not obligated to take her back. Skilled-nursing facilities are full and have at least a two-year waiting list. Even more detrimental, skilled-nursing facilities can only admit a small percentage of Medicaid patients due to the reduced fees paid by the government. Some skilled-nursing facilities do not accept Medicaid patients at all. Sometimes openings are in a different city or county. Family preferences are not taken into account.

As always, there are some exceptions to the rule. In some instances, a patient can get bumped up from a waiting list if they are transferring out of a hospital and require critical medical help provided by skilled nursing. That was how Mom originally got her skilled-nursing placement.

Of course, if you have an unlimited budget, you have unlimited options. But Mom's savings were dwindling from the sale of her property. When her funds ran out, her only option would be to apply for Medicaid.

We decided to leave Mom there as she had established her place. If she required Medicaid while being a skilled-nursing home patient, the facility was required to keep her. It was also a short driving distance from us. Luckily, Mom's savings lasted long enough for her to avoid applying for Medicaid.

Final Goodbye

Mom did not have to move again. Her long journey was over: two and a half years living with us, two years in residential care, and a year and a half in skilled nursing. On a Tuesday, I got a call from the skilled-nursing facility to let me know that Mom's vital signs showed her bodily systems were shutting down. She was in a coma.

Joe had recently purchased a plane ticket to visit us on Friday. I had heard that people in a coma could sometimes hear and understand conversations, so I whispered in her ear, "Hang on until Friday, Joe will be here so we all can say goodbye." And she did. Joe and I saw her Friday afternoon. At age ninety-two, Mom passed peacefully in her sleep

that night. She had lived for six years in California, always hoping she would return to her utopia in Tucson, Arizona.

Life Lessons

We were grateful that we had been able to make choices for Mom for a few years, at least. Although we would never have chosen this path for her last years, we learned a great deal while walking it with her. We have chosen to create this book as one way of sharing our experiences with others who may find themselves in these strange waters.

Following the path life gave us, we learned that we were stronger than we had expected. And we remain grateful for all the people who helped brighten Mom's final years. Thanks to all who loved her, visited her, took her on excursions, brought treats, and made meals. We are indebted to our village.

GAYLORD and SUSAN JOSEPH
BRANDON

TODD and DIANE FISHER
NATE, ALLIE, and MATTHEW

ROY and TONI BOLLINGER
ROYCE and ISSY

JOE RUBEL

RUSS and MAUREEN OPFER

BRUCE and LINDA HAGER

C H A P T E R   2

Write It Down

Have you memorized your doctor's name, phone number, and address? What about your dentist? Your vet? Do you keep one file with information about all your prescriptions?

Where do you keep your most important documents—like your passport or birth certificate? Where are your insurance policies? Do you have a will or a trust agreement? Where are they?

Who would you call if you had an accident and could not make it to the office tomorrow? Would you know which credit cards need to be canceled if you lose your wallet? Do your kids know which bank you use or where to find information about your retirement accounts?

More important, would family or friends be able to locate your important information in an emergency? What would happen if you are in a car wreck that leaves you unconscious—would your spouse or kids know how to find the answers to all the questions medical personnel and insurance agents will be asking?

The time to answer those questions is now—before an accident or illness leaves you or your loved ones scrambling to fill in the blanks. Throughout the planner, tables have been provided to help you organize your most important information and make it easier for family or friends to step in during an emergency. Use these tables to fill in the relevant information needed for every person in your household.

Important Personal Information

Personal information for

Item	Location	Comments
Address book	Shelf above computer	6 x 8 black, 3-ring binder
Birth certificate	Green lockbox in hall closet	Key hanging behind refrigerator
Address book		
Business contacts		
Birth certificate		
Death certificate		
Social Security card		
Marriage certificate		
Divorce papers		
Military papers Discharge DD214 form		
Passport		
Citizenship papers		
Church membership, baptismal records		
Community memberships		

Important Personal Information
(Continued)

Personal information for

Item	Location	Comments

Quick Reference Telephone Numbers

For quick reference, list contact phone numbers you would like to have easily available to you and your family.

Contact	Name	Phone number	Email address
Primary care doctor			
Dentist			
Beautician			
Barber			
Mechanic			
Tax preparer			
Financial planner			
Personal attorney			
Business attorney			
Insurance agent			
Stockbroker			
Electrician			
Plumber			
Heating, AC repair			
Handyperson			
Landlord			
Neighbor contact			
Neighbor contact			
Lawn care			
Gardener			

Quick Reference Telephone Numbers

(Continued)

Contact	Name	Phone number	Email address
Real estate agent			

Quick Reference Telephone Numbers

(Continued)

Contact	Name	Phone number	Email address

Financial Information

Financial information for

Item	Identification/ company	Information location	Account #	Phone #	Comments
Credit card					
Credit card					
Debit card					
Debit card					
Checking account					
Bank account					
Savings account					
Emergency account					
List of assets					
List of debts					
Mortgage					
Car loan					
Other loan(s)					

Financial Information

(Continued)

Financial information for

Item	Identification/ company	Information location	Account #	Phone #	Comments
Savings bonds					
Life insurance					
Accidental					
Annuities					
Employer					
Pension					
Veteran					
Car insurance					
Federal tax returns, past 3-5 years					
State tax returns, past 3-5 years					
Other investments					

Financial Information
(Continued)

Financial information for

Item	Identification/ company	Information location	Account #	Phone #	Comments

Personal Loan Granted

Person loan made to _____   Phone #: _____

Person granting loan _____   Phone # _____

Date of loan _____ $ loan amount _____

Date of payment	$ Payment	Loan balance	Date of payment	$ Payment	Loan balance

Personal Loan Received

Person loan made to _____ Phone #: _____

Person granting loan _____ Phone # _____

Date of loan _____ $ loan amount _____

Date of payment	$ Payment	Loan balance	Date of payment	$ Payment	Loan balance

Other Important Documents

List important information not included in auxiliary worksheets.

List document	Documents for	Information about document

Will or Trust

Information for

Location of will or trust

Do you have a will?   ☐ Yes   ☐ No

Do you have a trust?   ☐ Yes   ☐ No

Please circle which term applies (will or trust?) for your following documents.

Will or trust originated and signed date

Copy of will/trust given to, if applicable

Preparer of will or trust

Name   Title

Street address   City, state, zip

Phone   Email   Web

General power of attorney for finance   ☐ Yes   ☐ No

Durable power of attorney for finance   ☐ Yes   ☐ No

Will or Trust reviewed or revised date

Will or Trust reviewed or revised date

Executor of Will or Trustee of Trust

Name of Executor of an Estate
or
Name of Trustee of a Trust

Street address   City, state, zip

Phone number   Email

General Power of Attorney for Finance

A general power of attorney for finance is a legal document that authorizes an agent to make financial transactions for you. An authorized agent may sign checks, prepare tax returns, enter into contracts, buy or sell real estate, deposit and withdraw bank funds, and run a business for you.

A person authorizing an agent to act on his or her behalf by a power of attorney is known as the **principal**, **grantor**, or **donor** of the power.

Granting power of attorney for finance allows your agent to step into your shoes in financial situations, so grant this position to an attorney, trusted friend, or relative who understands finance. An agent can only exercise a power that you are able to do. For example, if you're in a coma and can't sign a contract, your agent can't sign either.

A power of attorney can be broad, limited, or tailored for a specific purpose, and an agent cannot act outside his/her designated scope. For example, if you plan to sell a home that you own in another state, you can grant power of attorney to an agent who lives in that state to sell your home. In this case, you would create a limited power of attorney, setting a specific date for the authorization to take effect. When the home is sold and all paperwork is completed, the relationship ends, and the agent no longer holds any power over your affairs.

A general power of attorney can be revoked by the grantor at any time as long as the grantor has legal capacity to act. A general power of attorney typically ends when (1) the purpose of power of attorney is completed, (2) the grantor becomes mentally unable to make coherent decisions, or (3) the grantor dies.

General Power of Attorney for Finance

Name of grantor _____ Date signed _____

Location of document _____

Appointed representative (agent) _____

Name _____

Street address _____

City, state, zip _____

Phone number _____

Email _____

Attorney/trust advisor generating power of attorney for finance, if applicable

Name _____

Business, if applicable _____

Street address _____

City, state, zip _____

Phone number _____

Email _____

Durable Power of Attorney for Finance

Like the general power of attorney for finance, a durable power of attorney is a legal document that authorizes an agent to make financial transactions for you. However, a durable power of attorney for finance begins when the document is signed and stays in effect for the grantor's lifetime.

The holder of the durable power of attorney can make financial decisions even when the grantor cannot, and decisions can be made without a court's permission.

A grantor, who has legal capacity to act, can revoke a durable power of attorney at any time.

In the event the grantor becomes incapacitated and unable to make decisions, a family member or business associate is entitled to petition the local probate court to be appointed a conservator of that person. If the need arises, the conservator then can petition the probate court to revoke the grantor's durable power of attorney.

Durable Power of Attorney for Finance

Name of grantor _____ Date signed _____

Location of document _____

Appointed representative (agent) _____

Name _____

Street address _____

City, state, zip _____

Phone number _____

Email _____

Attorney/trust advisor generating durable power of attorney for finance, if applicable

Name _____

Business, if applicable _____

Street address _____

City, state, zip _____

Phone number _____

Email _____

Vital Household Information

Running a household involves lots of documents and information. Much of that information is typically stored in your head or on receipts or contracts or scraps of paper tucked away in various drawers or folders. But what happens if you have an illness or an accident and someone else needs to take care of your bills or the routine house maintenance? Will they know where to look to find the needed information?

Use the forms on the next few pages to get all this routine information in one place. It will take a little time at first to write it all down, but it can save you time in the long run. And it can be invaluable to family or friends in case of emergency.

Household Bills, Maintenance Information

Item	Company name	Location	Account #	Phone #
Mortgage company				
Monthly payment	$	—	—	—
Second mortgage				
Monthly payment	$	—	—	—
Yearly taxes	$	—	—	—
Property deed				
Landlord				
Monthly rent	$	—	—	—
Rental agreement				
Real estate company				
Home security company				
Homeowner's insurance				
Insurance policy	$	—	—	—
Appliance contract				

Household Bills, Maintenance Information
(Continued)

Item	Company name	Location	Account #	Phone #
Appliance contract				
Appliance repair				
Storage locker				

Home Utilities Information

Company	Provider name	Account #	Phone #
Electric provider			
Gas provider			
Water provider			
Cable/internet provider			
Phone: landline provider			
Phone: cell provider			

Waste Management Information

Waste management provider

Phone #   Account #

Trash pickup

Circle:	# of barrels 1 2 3 4	Pickup day M T W TH F

Recycle pickup

Circle:	# of barrels 1 2 3 4	Pickup day M T W TH F

Yard waste pickup

Circle:	# of barrels 1 2 3 4	Pickup day M T W TH F

Solar Power Information

Solar company	Phone #	Contract #	Amount owed	Date	Payment	Balance

End-of-Life Care

End-of-life care is complicated. There are many decisions to be made and actions to take. If the patient and his/her family have an understanding of medical terminology and have completed the forms associated with healthcare, the transition to end-of-life medical care is manageable and allows the patient and his/her family some authority over his/her care.

Terminology and Forms

Do Not Resuscitate (DNR)

A DNR directive tells medical workers that a person does not want to be revived from unconsciousness or apparent death. This order deals exclusively with whether or not a person wishes to be revived if his/her breathing or heart stops. It should ensure that medical providers will not perform chest compressions, give drugs meant to restart the heart, or put a breathing tube in place.

Do Not Intubate (DNI)

A DNI directive means that medical personnel can attempt to revive a person with chest compressions and cardiac drugs, but they should not place any tubes, such as a tracheal tube for ventilation, in the person with the directive.

   DNR and DNI forms can be used with or without an advanced care directive or living will. Discuss your preferences with your physician; he/she can write the orders and place them in your medical records.

POLST (Portable Medical Order)

A POLST, also known as Physician Orders for Life-Sustaining Treatment, details the levels of medical intervention a person is comfortable with. In California, nurses, social workers, and religious leaders often play a role in initiating a POLST conversation, but a patient must express his/her wishes in a discussion with his/her doctor. A POLST form contains medical orders and must be signed by a physician.

   A POLST lets emergency and medical providers know if they should administer cardio-pulmonary resuscitation (CPR) in case of emergency. It should also explain whether a person wants to be fed by artificial means, including feeding tubes.

Tattoo a Legal Document?

A DNR tattoo is a dramatic way to make your wishes known. But will a DNR tattoo stop medical personnel from administering CPR?

Legal documentation from a doctor is required to support a DNR tattoo request. There have been news reports of a DNR tattoo being ignored by hospital staff. Treating a patient who has not presented proper legal paperwork can result in lawsuits, medical board reviews, and loss of license for hospitals and personnel.

A better choice is to wear a DNR wristband or neck medallion with the words "DO NOT RESUSCITATE" that also notes the whereabouts of legal paperwork. Inscribed jewelry is available for purchase in various places, including Amazon.

Get Legal Help

This is especially true for the following detailed medical forms: living will, DNR, DNI, POLST, and durable healthcare power of attorney.

Review advanced healthcare directives with your doctor(s), healthcare agent, alternative agents, and select family members. Provide them with a copy of completed directives.

Keep original forms in a safe place and carry a copy with you when you travel. Directives can be changed at any time by creating new forms. Destroy prior forms if you make changes so that your latest wishes will be clear.

Durable Healthcare Power of Attorney

A durable healthcare power of attorney provides instructions about your own healthcare. You are authorizing an agent to act on your behalf and legally you are known as the principal, grantor, or donor of the power. You must be eighteen or older to create this document, which will:

- Designate a representative (agent) to act on your behalf to make healthcare decisions if you are unable to do so.
- Give the selected agent the power to make any and all healthcare decisions if you become incapable of making those decisions.
- Allow your agent to make informed decisions about how to manage deathbed issues.

Durable Healthcare Power of Attorney

This is a powerful legal document. Consult a knowledgeable professional.

Name of grantor

Date signed

Location of durable healthcare power of attorney

Appointed representative (agent)

Name & title

Street address

City, state, zip

Phone number

Attorney/trust advisor/doctor generating durable healthcare power of attorney, if applicable.

Name

Business, if applicable

Street address

City, state, zip

Phone number

Email

Living Will

A living will (also known as an advance directive) is a written, legal document that spells out medical treatments you would and would not want to be used to keep you alive. It can also give instructions on other medical or health-related issues, such as what types of pain management you prefer and whether you would be willing to donate organs after death.

When creating a living will, you can leave specific instructions for how you want your family and medical caregivers to address numerous types of issues. You can provide advice about when to start or stop certain types of care or procedures and how you would like to be treated if you are in a coma or suffering from a terminal condition. Include these types of issues in your living will:

- resuscitation, including CPR
- mechanical ventilation
- feeding tubes
- antibiotics or antiviral medications
- dialysis
- organ, tissue, and body donations
- comfort or palliative care
- hospice care

A living will is limited to deathbed decisions. A doctor(s) must verify that the patient meets the following criteria:

- is unable to make his/her own medical decisions,
- is in a vegetative state,
- is unable to communicate his/her wishes,
- has a terminal illness, or
- cannot understand choices about medical care and effects.

You can have both a living will and a durable power of attorney for healthcare. You may include DNR or DNI orders in your living will. DNR or DNI can be prepared as separate forms, even if you don't create a full living will.

Living Will
This is a powerful legal document. Consult a knowledgeable professional.

Information for _____   Date signed _____

Location of living will _____

Attorney/trust advisor generating living will,
if applicable.

Name _____   Title _____

Firm _____

Street address _____

City, state, zip _____

Phone number _____   Email _____

Doctor generating medical forms.

Name _____   Medical practice _____

Street address _____

City, state, zip _____

Phone number _____

Email _____

Living Will

This is a powerful legal document. Consult a knowledgeable professional.

(Continued)

Healthcare form	Patient has Yes or No	Filed in medical records Yes or No	Filed with living will Yes or No	Date origination of document
Physician orders for life-sustaining treatment				
Healthcare directives				
Registered organ donor				
DNR Do not resuscitate				
DNI Do not intubate				
Durable Healthcare Power of Attorney				

Vital Healthcare Information

Doctors. Dentists. Optometrists. Therapists. Test results. Health records.

As you get older, you may feel like you spend a lot of time shuffling from one appointment to the next, and you may have accumulated quite a collection of contact information for medical specialists and therapist's offices. If you keep all that information in one place, you will be less likely to wind up at the physical therapist's office when you intended to go to the podiatrist.

You will also find it helpful to keep a record not only of upcoming appointments but also of past medical appointments. It is hard to remember exactly when you received particular vaccines or other medical procedures.

A log helps you track needed information so you can see at a glance whether it's been six months or six years since your last vision check or flu shot.

And, of course, leaving records like this can be a literal lifesaver in an emergency. If family or friends are able to quickly contact the doctors who know you best, you are more likely to get the best appropriate care.

List of Medical Providers

Patient name

Name of doctor	Specialty	Address	Phone #	First seen

Log of Doctor Visits

Patient name

Name of doctor	Appointment date	Next appointment	Diagnosis, results, comments

Log of Dentist Visits

Patient name

Name of dentist	Appointment date	Next appointment	Diagnosis, results, comments

Log of Medical Visits, Procedures

EXAMPLE LOG

Date	Doctor/ Healthcare provider	Procedure	Notes
4/22/2019	Urgent Care	Tetanus/diphtheria/ pertussis vaccine.	Stepped on rusty nail while gardening. Did not have a record of last tetanus shot. Dr. highly recommended latest vaccine with whooping cough protection.
6/14/2019	CVS Pharmacy	Received flu shot/high dose.	Good for 1 year.
10/09/19	Dr. Jane Smith	Received shingles vaccine (2 shots required). Shingrix 1st shot 10/09/19.	Shingrix 2nd shot scheduled for 02/12/20. Vaccine is given four months apart.
11/07/19	Rolling Oaks Radiology	Mammogram and bone density test. Mammogram report. All good. Bone density low. Recommendation to take calcium every day and lift weights.	Reschedule mammogram in 1 year. Bone density in 2.

Log of Medical Visits, Procedures

Patient name

Date	Doctor/ Healthcare provider	Procedure	Notes

Log of Medical Visits, Procedures

(Continued)

Patient name

Date	Doctor/ Healthcare provider	Procedure	Notes

Drug Information
Prescription and Over the Counter

Drug interactions can cause a wide array of results—most of them bad. Keeping track of medications and letting medical personnel know what you are taking is key to getting good healthcare. Any doctor who is writing a prescription for you should be provided a list of every prescription you are taking, as well as the vitamins, supplements, and over-the-counter remedies.

Use the charts on the following pages to keep track of what drugs you are taking. And read the story of Tom and Betty to see why it's so important to update your lists regularly.

Tom and Betty—Word M (Medication)

Betty's husband, Tom, took a newly prescribed drug for high blood pressure—we'll call it Medication A—shortly before going to bed one night. During the middle of the night, Tom grew deathly ill. He was gasping for breath, pale, drenched in sweat. Was he having a heart attack?

Shaky and worried about Tom, Betty wondered whether she was capable of driving him to the hospital and thought about calling paramedics instead. Knowing the hospital was close, Betty mustered her courage and drove Tom to the emergency room, weakly whispering, "Yay. Made it," as they arrived.

After hours of waiting, paperwork, and tests, Tom received his diagnosis: **"Allergy to Medication A."**

Five years later, a different physician prescribed "Medication A" for Tom. Knowing the prescription name sounded vaguely familiar, Tom checked his list of drugs taken and reactions and realized what had happened the last time he had taken that particular blood pressure medication. He declared, "POISON," and wisely refused the prescription. Tom's documentation prevented a reoccurrence of the nightmarish ER visit—*or worse*.

Prescriptions, Over-the-Counter Medicine, Vitamins

Individual's name

Date	Name of drug, vitamin, supplement	RX #	Name, specialty, phone # of prescribing doctor	Results and reactions
			_____ _____ _____	
			_____ _____ _____	
			_____ _____ _____	
			_____ _____ _____	
			_____ _____ _____	

Prescriptions, Over-the-Counter Medicine, Vitamins
(Continued)

Individual's name

Date	Name of drug, vitamin, supplement	RX #	Name, specialty, phone # of prescribing doctor	Results and reactions
			_____ _____ _____	
			_____ _____ _____	
			_____ _____ _____	
			_____ _____ _____	
			_____ _____ _____	

Insurance

Insurance is a necessary part of life—especially as you get older. And it's not easy to keep track of all the ins and outs of various policies and coverages. That's why it's so important to record your information in easy-to-find, easy-to-use lists and logs like the ones you will find on the following pages.

You will also find a log that will let you keep track of which insurance policies are accepted at various hospitals, nursing homes, or other healthcare providers.

If you have Medicare insurance, be sure your doctor or medical facility is a Medicare provider. If your procedure, doctor, or medical facility is not Medicare approved, you are responsible for the full bill.

Medical Insurance Plans

Name of insured

	Policy ID#	Policy started	Yearly deductible amount	Notes
Medicare A				
Medicare B				
Medicare C HMO				
Medicare C PPO				
Medicare D				
Medigap				
Kaiser				

Medical Insurance Plans
(Continued)

Name of insured

	Policy ID#	Policy started	Yearly deductible amount	Notes
Work coverage				
Private insurance				
Primary insurer				
Secondary				
Dental				
Eye				
Health savings				

Medical Insurance Plans
(Continued)

Name of insured

	Policy ID#	Policy started	Yearly deductible amount	Notes

Insurance Accepted by Specific Facilities

List medical facilities approved by your insurance plan such as
Blue Cross, Medicare, Medi-Cal, Kaiser, etc. Record if certain facilities do not accept
your insurance or no insurance.

Patient name

Name of facility	Address	Phone #	Name accepted insurance(s)	Our insurance not accepted

Pet Care

Not all members of our households are human. Dogs, cats, birds, and various other animals need care, too, and that care can get complicated in emergencies or when friends or family members don't have access to the necessary information.

Use the logs on the following pages to help get all the vital pet care information in one place. Read Rusty's story to see how complicated and confusing these situations can be. And if you are lucky enough to have found a compassionate, budget-friendly veterinarian, share the knowledge with all your friends!

Rusty's Transition

2:30 p.m. Bill, who was suffering from Alzheimer's disease, had been living with a caretaker since his wife's death. When Rusty, Bill's twelve-year-old canine companion, died one Sunday afternoon, the caretaker did not know what to do, so he called Bill's friend Tom.

2:45 p.m. Tom conferred with his daughter, who recommended a local vet. Tom called the veterinarian's office, explained the situation, and asked if they would pick up Rusty at Bill's house. "No, we do not offer pickup services. The office closes at 5:00 p.m. If we are to take care of Rusty, the dog needs to be here before then. The cost to take care of remains will be $250. Has Rusty ever seen our vet?" Tom didn't know but supplied Bill's name and phone number. Luckily, he learned that the vet had treated Rusty previously; thus, the cost of dealing with Rusty's remains dropped from $250 to $120.

3:00 p.m. Tom drove to Bill's home. Another friend of Bill's was called to sit with Bill and distract him while Tom and the caretaker wrapped the ninety-pound dog in bags and lugged him to the car. Not a pretty sight. Tom, eighty-one, would have preferred to be reading about this process rather than taking part.

4:50 p.m. Tom, caretaker, and deceased dog arrived at the vet's office ten minutes before closing.

Rusty's story illustrates how last-minute phone calls to friends and vets are not optimal choices when dealing with an ill or deceased pet. In hindsight and for future reference, Tom discovered that a nearby county animal shelter offers services to pick up and dispose of dead animals for fees based on weight. Keep information about your community shelter nearby in case you have a similar need.

Name of local animal shelter

Phone number

Other options. There are private businesses that will pick up bodies of pets or transport living pets for various reasons and appointments. Many of these businesses operate 24/7. Check your community resources to find such a service in your area.

General Pet Care Information

	Name	Phone #	Email
Current veterinarian			
Option 2 veterinarian			
Pet sitter			
Pet sitter			
Dog walker			
Dog walker			

Pet Information Log

Pet name   Type of pet   Birthdate

Relevant information (special food, allergies, medical conditions)

Vaccination Record

Pet's name	Vet's name	Date	Type of vaccination

Pet Medical Record

Pet name	Veterinarian facility	Phone #	Reason	Visit date	Results

Pet Medical Record

(Continued)

Pet name	Veterinarian facility	Phone #	Reason	Visit date	Results

Pet Care Contacts

In event of owner's emergency, illness, or death.

Animal name	Person responsible for animal care	Address	Phone #
		_____ _____ _____	
		_____ _____ _____	
		_____ _____ _____	
		_____ _____ _____	
		_____ _____ _____	
		_____ _____ _____	
		_____ _____ _____	

Important Dates

We have created lists and logs and handy guides throughout most of this chapter to help you get all your information organized and in one place. But an inexpensive "month at a glance" calendar will be your best bet to help you keep track of important dates. You can use the calendar to record future appointments and also dates and events you want to recall annually. Make sure your family knows where to find your calendar in case there's an emergency.

Use a calendar to record:

- Birthdays: on the date, include the name, age, and any other relevant information about the person who is celebrating
- Anniversaries: date, name, number of years married
- Camping dates
- Vacations
- Bill due dates: utilities, vehicle loans, mortgage, etc.
- DMV license renewal dates: recreation vehicles, autos, include cost for each
- State and federal taxes: due dates
- Due dates for property taxes
- Home improvements: track age of item each year
- Medical/vision/dental appointments
- Pension/work wages/Social Security monthly income
- Bank CD amounts and maturity dates
- Magazines/newspaper/memberships: due dates
- Holidays
- Additional information relevant to your daily life

Post important events to your calendar. Each month, circle items that have been completed. Anything not circled for a particular month is unfinished business.

Save your completed calendar for historical reference. At the beginning of each year, retrieve important information for the year to come by referring to events and dates listed in the previous year's calendar.

If appropriate, carry a small pocket-size calendar. Enter important dates when out and about and then transfer them to your larger calendar when you get home.

Of course, paper calendars are rather old school. The "new and improved" calendar method is logging information into a smartphone calendar. Your phone can then

alert you of upcoming events and appointments, and you can share your calendar with others. But it's hard to beat a paper calendar for ease of use. It's usually easier to see "at a glance" what's coming up or what you've accomplished.

CHAPTER 3

Passwords, User Names, Security Questions, Subscriptions, and Subscription Services

Creating an alphabetized list of all internet accounts, user names, passwords, and security questions and answers can be an important time-saver as more and more of your important information can be accessed online.

In addition to bank accounts, utilities, and cable access, more and more doctors, healthcare providers, and hospitals are allowing patients the ability to access medical information online. This kind of access can be invaluable when you are helping a loved one—and it can even allow you to get healthcare information about a family member who lives far away from you. But you must know that the information is available online, how to get to that website, the user name, and password of the account in question.

Use the tips in this chapter to help you create secure passwords and to remember that information. Then be sure to share the access information with your most important accounts with loved ones who could be called on to help you in an emergency.

The Password Nightmare

How hard can it be to keep up with passwords for your online accounts? It's simple, right? A website asks for a password. I type a series of numbers and letters easily remembered. How confusing can it be?

Well, let's see how that goes.
Tuesday, January 22, 2019

Me	Open ABC website.
ABC website	Choices: Sign in or new account?
Me	I select new account.
ABC website	Fill in user name and password.
Me	User name: Sally Smart; password: pass123
ABC website	Password too weak. Must be at least eight characters.
Me	Oh, fudge. I have used pass123 many times; easy to remember. I type password: pass1234
ABC website	Password too weak. Needs a symbol, capital letter.
Me	I type the password: Pass#1234
ABC website	Confirm.
Me	Hooray. This is easy to remember. I'm late picking up the kids. I write user name and password on this piece of paper right by my desk.

Wednesday, January 23, 2019

Me	Open ABC website.
ABC website	Request: User name and password.
Me	I type user name: Sally Smart and password: pass#1234
ABC website	Wrong user name or password.
Me	Unbelievable. What did I use as my user name? Did I use a name or email address? Sometimes websites ask for an email address when you first sign up. I'm positive I used Sally Smart as my user name and originated the password as pass#1234. I'll try again. Didn't I write this down somewhere? Where is that piece of paper? Oh, here it is. Of course, I need a capital P! I type user name: Sally Smart; Password: Pass#1234. Yay! I'm in.

Yes, creating a user name and password *should* be simple, but this simple task can feel overwhelming if you are relying on slips of paper around the computer to help you remember all the information. Also, it is helpful to have a list of preplanned passwords ready *before* creating new accounts; it will help you avoid a time crunch and remember what you created.

Themed Password Books

Amazon has many types and styles of password books in all price ranges for purchase. The idea is to use a book with a cute cover that appeals to your interests but is not easily recognized as a password cheat sheet to others. Your goal is to be able to have this information in a convenient format and location that won't be so easily spotted by others.

Some of the themes for password books are Buddha, Paris, cats, dogs, etc. They range in price from about $5 to around $20. I use a small, six-ring binder with A-Z index tabs, as it is easy to add clean pages and remove pages with multiple crossed-out entries.

A password book can make a fantastic holiday, Mother's Day, Father's Day, or birthday gift, especially for an older parent. An added bonus to your gift would be for you and the receiver to fill in the information together. Or maybe you can create one with your information and give it to one of your kids so that they will have easy access to your accounts if needed.

Keep a copy of your most important passwords and estate information off-site in case of fire or earthquakes.

Password Book Tips

Organize and locate all necessary information using the templates on the following pages as your guide.

- Notify the person(s) assuming your responsibilities in the event of illness or death where to locate the information.
- Keep a copy at a different address with a trusted friend or relative.
- Keep a copy with your estate plan.

If you would rather not go buy a password book, use the following worksheets to track your online accounts. Keep them in a loose-leaf notebook.

Internet Accounts

User Name, PIN or Password, Security Questions, Security Answers

Website name	User name	PIN or password	Security questions	Security answers

Subscriptions, Online Plans, Warranties

Recently checking my bank statement, I was upset to discover the price for an online software subscription I purchased had risen from $9.99 to $14.99 a month without any notification. Then came surprise two. An online subscription had added an extra product to an existing account—for an additional $9.99 monthly fee!

Are you surprised to know that once you subscribe to a service it may automatically renew every year? Your dad who no longer watches television may have a monthly basic cable service bill, plus premium channels. Payments for this service may be automatically taken out of his checking or credit account and will continue until cancellation. He may not even be aware that this service has gone up considerably since his promotional subscription. For years, he may pay for unneeded and unused services.

Microsoft recently sent me a friendly reminder that my yearly subscription to Microsoft 365 would be renewing shortly. I was given the date and dollar amount of the renewal. *So appreciated. Kudos to Microsoft.* All companies should be responsible and offer this courtesy service.

Confusing! Difficult! And even more maddening if you are dealing with someone else's subscriptions! To make it more challenging, a majority of companies no longer simply offer telephone contact numbers. Instead a customer must go through an online chat room service. Unbelievable how much fun that is.

Hats off to Apple. Apple's support number is easily found by Googling. You can actually talk to a live person on the phone and receive helpful, friendly assistance.

Subscriptions, Online Plans, Warranties
EXAMPLE LOG

Use these logs to help keep track of your subscriptions and warranties and other relevant information. It will save time and aggravation in the long run!

Company providing service	Toyota	Subscription service warranty	Extended warranty
Starting	3/30/18	**Ending**	3/30/25
Phone #	1-800-xxx-xxxx	**Website**	Toyota#1.com
Comments	7 years/100,000 miles with zero deductible		

Subscriptions, Online Plans, Warranties

Use these logs to help keep track of your subscriptions and warranties and other relevant information. It will save time and aggravation in the long run!

Company
providing service

Subscription
service warranty

Starting

Ending

Phone #

Website

Comments

Company
providing service

Subscription
service warranty

Starting

Ending

Phone #

Website

Comments

Company
providing service

Subscription
service warranty

Starting

Ending

Phone #

Website

Comments

Company
providing service

Subscription
service warranty

Starting

Ending

Phone #

Website

Comments

Company
providing service

Subscription
service warranty

Starting

Ending

Phone #

Website

Comments

Subscriptions, Online Plans, Warranties

(Continued)

Company
providing service   Subscription
                                                          service warranty

Starting   Ending

Phone #   Website

Comments

Company
providing service   Subscription
                                                          service warranty

Starting   Ending

Phone #   Website

Comments

Company
providing service   Subscription
                                                          service warranty

Starting   Ending

Phone #   Website

Comments

Company
providing service   Subscription
                                                          service warranty

Starting   Ending

Phone #   Website

Comments

Company
providing service   Subscription
                                                          service warranty

Starting   Ending

Phone #   Website

Comments

## CHAPTER 4

Staying on Top of Bills and Payments

Paying bills is one of the most routine, necessary tasks for any household. But illness or declining memory can make this chore far more challenging. Family members forced to step in to pay bills after a death or medical emergency can find this undertaking incredibly daunting.

Take charge of your finances now by getting into the habit of logging income and expenses. It will be far easier to keep track of everything when all the information is in one place and a blessing to family or business associates in an emergency.

When you log your bill information, there will be no doubt about what household bills are due or when the last payment was made. If your family ever wonders whether you're taking care of things as you should, one glance at your logs will help them rest easy. And if an emergency arises, anyone can step in and keep the household running with the least amount of disruption possible. And using bill-paying logs will also provide a sense of accountability, proving to all involved where the money has gone.

Ready-made accounting-ledger income and expense books are available from any office supply store, or you can find a wide variety of styles and types on Amazon. It is helpful to know what works and what doesn't by reading the Amazon reviews on the product you select. A few homemade computer tables have been added to this chapter to give you an idea of what it looks like when keeping track of payments this way. Develop your own style and method, but it's helpful to always include name of bill owed, date, amount, and how the bill was paid.

In the Dark

Keeping financial records of household expenses will help avoid the plight of Mary and her daughter, Kim. Mary and Dan had been married for twenty-five years and were living comfortably. Dan was proud of their 760 FICO score and lack of debt. Mary didn't know or care what a FICO score was.

One Sunday morning, Dan drove his Mercedes-Benz convertible to the beach to paddleboard. It was an awesome day. No wind, water smooth as glass. Although he was pushing sixty, Dan paddled most Sunday mornings. It gave him a feeling of serenity, of being one with God and nature. After his jaunt, he would meet Mary for brunch.

That Sunday, Mary arrived at their normal spot and ordered breakfast for both of them. She waited and waited. After drinking a Bloody Mary and then another, Mary acknowledged people were waiting for their seats and anxious to be seated. Their no-longer scrumptious breakfasts were boxed to go. She was miffed. Dan was always punctual. At home, she checked her answering machine looking for a clue as to why she had been stood up.

That's when she learned about the terrible crash on Pacific Coast Highway caused by a wrong-way driver. Her vivacious husband, who always took care of her, would not be meeting her for breakfast ever again.

Kim drove home from UC Berkeley to help, although it was a busy time during her senior year in college. Inheriting her dad's analytical skills, Kim envisioned quickly comforting her mom, setting a temporary budget, arranging her dad's memorial, then returning quickly to school. She loved her parents and was feeling extreme sorrow, but she had worked hard the last three years of college and did not want to get off track despite the horrid, unbelievable distractions in her life.

After Dan's memorial, Mary baked Kim a cherry pie. It had always been Kim and Dan's favorite. Mary started to cry missing Dan and knowing he would not be sharing. Kim enjoyed the pie but thought it was strange that her mom had asked to be taken to the store so she could get cherry pie filling, when Kim knew there were five jars in the pantry.

After finals, Kim returned home and dug in, trying to sort the mail from the piles all over her dad's desk. She was shocked to discover her mother had thrown out some of the mail because it had been addressed to Dan.

"Mom, why would you do that?"

"Don't be silly, Kim. Your dad is no longer here. Why should we keep his mail?"

Unfortunately, Mary's evaluation of her husband dying and not needing his mail is very common thinking by a person suffering with Alzheimer's.

Kim then worked on balancing the checkbook. Mary could not answer one question Kim asked about finances.

Later that night the wind howled, and the power suddenly went off.

Mary said, "Kim, darling, please turn on the lights, I can't see."

"Sorry, Mom, we have no electricity. Use the flashlight by your bed. I'll call the power company tomorrow, and we will know what's going on."

Ten minutes later, Mary asked again. "Kim, turn on the lights. I can't see. I'm cold and have to go to the bathroom. I don't know why you came to help me if you won't even turn on the lights?"

"Mom, I already told you I can't do anything until tomorrow. Please, please go to sleep."

Five minutes later, Mary began shouting, "SOMEONE TURN ON THE DAMN LIGHTS!"

After a *loooong* night, Kim phoned the electric company and discovered the power had been shut off not because of the weather but because the account had not been paid—despite the "past-due notice" that had been sent to Dan and Mary. Kim asked to be transferred to the billing department.

"I'm at my family home and the electricity has been turned off. Things are confusing," Kim explained. "My dad passed away. Apparently, my mother needs to make a payment."

The billing clerk replied, "I need to talk to your mother and verify this is her account."

Kim asked, "Is that really necessary? She is confused. We were up half the night; she is resting."

"Sorry. Our utility company is mandated to follow data privacy guidelines. I cannot talk to you without permission from the holder of the account, which is your mom. For future reference, you can obtain information about this account if your mother files a form to authorize us to release information to you."

Preventing Shutoffs

Utilities are often shut off because customers do not have the money to pay bills, but shutoffs can occur in cases like Mary's when customers miss payments because of family emergencies or creeping cognitive problems. If the power is shut off, the customer must pay the past-due amount or set up a payment plan to restore power. A new deposit may be required.

To help prevent shutoffs in cases like Mary's, most utility companies have some kind of "friendly reminder program" allowing a residential customer to designate a friend,

family member, or public/private agency to receive notices of upcoming bills and alerts if payments are late or missing. If Mary had set up such a reminder, Kim would have been notified that payment was past due—BEFORE the lights went out. Check with your utility companies to verify if they have a program and enroll yourself and your loved ones. It can be a real light-saver!

It's a good idea to authorize a friend or family member to discuss your accounts with utility companies, banks, credit card companies, mortgage companies, lenders, etc. Most of these organizations have simple release forms you can fill out and sign. It's an easy way to make sure you don't put one of your family members through Kim's nightmare!

Sample logs have been included with this chapter for your information and use.

Bills and Method of Payments, January–June

EXAMPLE LOG

Insurance, Health	Date amount January	Date amount February	Date amount March	Date amount April	Date amount May	Date amount June	How paid
Social Security Medicare, husband	1/2/19 $125.00	2/2/19 $125.00	3/2/19 $125.00	4/3/19 $125.00	5/2/19 $125.00	6/2/19 $125.00	Automatically from Social Security check.
Social Security Medicare, wife	1/2/19 $125.00	2/2/19 $125.00	3/2/19 $125.00	4/3/19 $125.00	5/2/19 $125.00	6/2/19 $125.00	Automatically from Social Security check.
USAA Health, Plan F husband	1/2/19 $218	2/2/19 $218	3/2/19 $218	4/3/19 $218	5/2/19 $218	6/2/19 $218	Paid auto-pay. Premier America checking.
USAA Health, Plan F wife	1/2/19 $207.00	2/2/19 $207.00	3/2/19 $207.00	4/3/19 $207.00	5/2/19 $207.00	6/2/19 $207.00	Paid auto-pay. Premier America checking.
Long-term care CNA husband	1/2/19 $1,200.00						Paid once a year by check.

Bills and Method of Payments, January–June

EXAMPLE LOG

(Continued)

Insurance, Health	Date amount January	Date amount February	Date amount March	Date amount April	Date amount May	Date amount June	How paid
Long-term care CNA wife	1/2/19 $800.00						Paid once a year by check.
Humana-Walmart drug, husband	1/2/19 $15.10	2/2/19 $15.10	3/2/19 $15.10	4/3/19 $15.10	5/2/19 $15.10	6/2/19 $15.10	Automatically from Social Security.
Humana-Walmart drug, wife	1/2/19 $15.10	2/2/19 $15.10	3/2/19 $15.10	4/3/19 $15.10	5/2/19 $15.10	6/2/19 $15.10	Automatically from Social Security.

Bills and Method of Payments, January–June

EXAMPLE LOG

Insurance, Home Cars/ Vehicles	Date amount January	Date amount February	Date amount March	Date amount April	Date amount May	Date amount June	How paid
State Farm home insurance	1/2/19 $900						Auto-pay Union Bank. Paid once a year.
State Farm umbrella insurance	1/2/19 $450.00						Auto-pay Union Bank. Paid once a year.
GeoVera earthquake insurance	1/2/19 $1,002.00						Paid once a year. Auto-pay American Express.

Bills and Method of Payments, January–June
EXAMPLE LOG
(Continued)

Insurance, Home Cars/ Vehicles	Date amount January	Date amount February	Date amount March	Date amount April	Date amount May	Date amount June	How paid
State Farm insurance, BMW	1/2/19 $1,320.00						Paid twice a year. Call and pay using American Express.
State Farm insurance, Ford truck	1/2/19 $950.00						Paid twice a year. Call and pay using American Express.
Progressive insurance, RV Monaco	1/2/19 $450.00						Paid twice a year. Call and pay using American Express.
AAA Club	1/2/19 $130.00						Paid once a year. Call and pay using American Express.
Good Neighbor Sam							No payment, canceled.

Bills and Method of Payments, January–June

EXAMPLE LOG

Some utilities are on level pay plan. Yearly amount averaged and paid per month.

Utilities	Date amount January	Date amount February	Date amount March	Date amount April	Date amount May	Date amount June	How paid
Southern California Gas	1/2/19 $55.00	2/2/19 $55.00	3/2/19 $55.00	4/2/19 $55.00	5/2/19 $55.00	6/2/19 $55.00	Monthly average. Auto-pay. Premier America checking.
Southern California Edison	1/2/19 $65.00	2/2/19 $65.00	3/2/19 $65.00	4/2/19 $65.00	5/2/19 $65.00	6/2/19 $65.00	Monthly average. Auto-pay. Premier America checking.
Las Virgenes Municipal Water District		2/2/19 $150.00		4/2/19 $150.00		6/2/19 $150.00	Every 2 months. Bimonthly average. Premier America checking.
GI Industries/ Waste Management	1/2/19 $49.00	2/2/19 $49.00	3/2/19 $49.00	4/2/19 $49.00	5/2/19 $49.00	6/2/19 $49.00	Monthly average. Auto-pay. Premier America checking.
Debit/Credit Cards: Capital One Master Card				4/16/19 $800.00			Wells Fargo checking. Only use 6 times per year to avoid annual fee.
Citibank Visa	1/2/19 $2,589.18	2/2/19 $3,778.33	3/2/19 $900.00	4/2/19 $5,557.00	5/2/19 $1,222.40	6/2/19 $4,336.99	Wells Fargo checking. Monthly auto-pay. Pay full balance owed.

Bills and Method of Payments, January–June

Make copies and use for your personal information.

Category	Date amount January	Date amount February	Date amount March	Date amount April	Date amount May	Date amount June	How paid

Bills and Method of Payments, July–December

Make copies and use for your personal information.

Category	Date amount July	Date amount August	Date amount September	Date amount October	Date amount November	Date amount December	How paid

CHAPTER 5

The Taxing Questions of Homeownership

California has many unique laws, regulations, and propositions regarding homeownership. Be aware that propositions can and do change often. With all the money spent and lost with Covid-19, California state and city governments are thinking of every possible way to raise tax money. This chapter provides a brief overview of two significant California propositions regarding taxes and homeownership. Please understand that there are many nuances to the laws and many exceptions and exemptions that can affect your ability to benefit from some of the items. Talk to a lawyer or a real estate expert before you finalize plans that hinge on any tax benefits. You can also verify information and obtain forms from your local county assessor's office. Each county in the state of California has its own office.

Proposition 13

Since the voters passed Proposition 13 in 1978, the value of a California residential home for property tax purposes is reassessed to market level only when a change in ownership takes place. The first year, new property owners pay property taxes of 1.1% of the sale price, plus any bonds or fees approved by voters. Following the first year, the value of the property tax is allowed to rise by a maximum of 2% per year over the previous year's tax bill. But again, your tax bill for any given year can be higher than 2% if any extra bonds or fees have been approved by voters.

California property taxes are high, but they would be even higher for many people without this 2% cap. Many senior citizens are able to stay in their homes because of Prop. 13.

Proposition 19

California Proposition 19 was passed by voters in the November 2020 election. Proposition 19 replaces former Propositions 58, 60, 90, and 193. Effective April 1, 2021, Proposition 19 allows homeowners who are eligible to transfer his/her primary residence property tax base to a replacement residence of any value, anywhere in California. Requirements needed to take advantage of this extension of Proposition 13 include being over the age of 55, severely disabled, or a person whose home was destroyed by wildfire or disaster. An eligible homeowner is allowed to take their current tax base with them when selling their personal residence and buying a new residential property. A homeowner who is over 55 or severely disabled may be eligible to use this tax advantage up to three times in his/her lifetime.

Effective February 16, 2021, a child or grandchild who is eligible to inherit a personal residence from his/her parents, or if the parents are deceased, grandparents, has one year to establish the inherited property as his/her personal residence to take advantage of using the parents or grandparents tax rate. If the child or grandchild does not use the inherited home as his/her personal residence within a year, the inherited home property tax will be reassessed to market value.

Caveat: A property tax bill for an inherited home or farm would go up if the price the property could be sold for exceeds the property's taxable value by more than $1 million (adjusted for inflation every two years). Unfortunately, in California, $1 million for a personal residence is not uncommon.

Selling a Home: Capital Gains Tax

When property is purchased and later sold, taxes are owed for the amount of profit made from the purchase and sale. This is known as a capital gains tax, and it is usually a considerable amount of money. It is important to correctly calculate a capital gain or loss from the sale of owned property to prevent a huge tax liability. Sometimes this calculation is a capital loss, not gain. Sorry, a capital loss does not entitle a deduction in taxes on taxes owed.

How do you calculate whether a purchased property has a capital gain or loss when sold? Subtract adjusted cost basis from adjusted sales basis to get your capital gain or loss.

Length of Ownership

Capital assets can be taxed at short-term or long-term rates. Once a capital gain or loss has been established, your next step is to consider length of ownership.

- **Short-term** refers to an asset owned for 365 days or less. Short-term capital gains are taxed at the same rate as regular income.
- **Long-term** capital assets are owned longer than 365 days and are taxed at a reduced rate depending on income levels.

Sale of Personal Residence

Federal and state tax liability is reduced for owners who are selling a house that has been their primary residence for two of the five years prior to sale and if it has been at least two years since a tax gain from another home sale has been used to reduce taxes. The IRS tax deduction from the profit of sale of a personal residence is $250,000 for a single person or $500,000 for a married couple.

A surviving spouse has different tax liability options. The widow or widower has two years from the date of their spouse's death to receive a $500,000 tax exclusion from the profit of sale of the couple's primary residence. After two years, the surviving spouse will be entitled only to the $250,000 tax exclusion.

Capital Property Improvements

When selling property, the cost of property improvements (not upkeep or maintenance) may be subtracted from tax gains. The IRS defines a capital improvement as a home improvement that adds market value to the home, prolongs its useful life, or adapts it to new uses.

Maintain your records as you go so you will not forget or lose pertinent information. Attach the following log to a file or manila folder, and keep all receipts and information inside.

Real Estate Purchase, Improvements Logs

Title holder(s) of property

Street address

City, state, zip   County

Date	Purchase price	Escrow fees	Other costs/fees	Initial real estate tax deduction not taken year of purchase	Primary	Vacation	Investment	Rental

Substantial Additions. Improvements. Do Not Include Repairs.
Keep All Receipts.

Date	Improvements	Company responsible for improvements	Expenses

Adjusted Cost Basis Example Worksheet
Sale of Personal Residence

Please remember this chart is subject to federal and state tax qualifications.

Purchase price of property	$500,000
Escrow fees	1,200
Related costs & fees	500
Initial real estate tax not taken year of purchase	4,000

Money spent on improvements that increased the value of the asset, such as a new room addition. Do not include repairs.

Kitchen remodel	30,000
Room addition	130,000
New roof	40,000
Solar installation	50,000
Total adjusted cost basis	**$755,700**

Adjusted Sales Basis

Please remember this chart is subject to federal and state tax qualifications.

Selling price of property	**$1,150,000**
Minus tax deductions	
Escrow fees	-6,000
Real estate commissions	-30,000
Qualifying selling costs	-400
Total adjusted sales basis	$1,113,600
Minus total adjusted cost basis	-755,700
Taxable profit	**$357,900**

If Qualified, Tax Exclusion from Taxable Profit

Please remember this chart is subject to federal and state tax qualifications.

Single Person Return

Taxable profit from home sale	**$357,900**
Minus single person tax exclusion	-250,000
Taxable Profit	**$107,900**

Joint Return

Taxable profit from home sale	$357,900
Minus joint return exclusion	-500,000
Taxable Profit	**-0-**

Knowing information about propositions and documenting expenses you have incurred in upgrading your home is essential. Chapter 2, "Write It Down!" demonstrates the key to success in financial management is to have a clear trail of paperwork. Without it, your work and knowledge are worth nothing.

A note about home improvements. With the housing shortage, the requirements have been relaxed in California to obtain permits to add an addition to your home, convert your garage, or build a granny flat. The new or renovated square footage of your home will be reassessed to market value as of the date of completion of construction. This will increase your property tax. Your property tax assessment on your home, except for the new construction, stays the same.

The Taxman Cometh

Once you have completed your tax returns, put them in a place that is secure but accessible to others. Following is a scenario of what may happen when your tax records cannot be found.

Will the IRS or the state Franchise Tax Board care you have twice searched every nook and cranny of Mom's house and can't locate last year's tax records or the information needed to file this year's taxes? Will they say, "Sorry, dear, all will be OK. We understand your tremendous anxiety. Your dad died. You flew from New York to California to help your sick mom. All tax records for Mom and Dad have vanished"? Or will you hear, "Oh, so sad. Back and current taxes must be paid even after death. Dying is not an excuse, and, by the way, expect to pay a penalty for late filing."

To avoid this scenario, it is helpful to know that, if needed, transcripts and copies of past tax returns are available from the IRS and your state's Franchise Tax Board.

Home Title

Whose name is on your home title? John had a small home and asked Sally to move in and share it with him. Sally and John lived happily together for more than 30 years. They lived the good life in sunny California. Surfing in the summer, skiing in the winter. They took extravagant vacations and had fun. They never married. When John died, his trust left everything to Sally, including his house, their home.

Sally transferred title to her name as required by law. She was surprised when her tax bill came and instead of the expected $2,036 yearly property tax, she was staring at a bill for yearly property taxes owed for $5,575. A 174% increase from last year. How could this be?

The answer is Sally would have had to be John's legal wife for her to qualify for Proposition 13 tax relief after his death. This would have been only a 2% increase over the previous year's tax bill. As soon as the property was transferred into her name, a non-legal spouse, the tax bill was assessed at the current market value of the house, making her tax bill $5,575 instead of $2,036. To keep the current tax rate when a person passes away, the beneficiary would have to be a spouse or child of the deceased.

CHAPTER 6

Navigating the Retirement Account Labyrinth

Retirement account rules and regulations change often, have many interpretations, are confusing, and are full of contradictions: if, and, but, unless, exceptions. This chapter is included only for general information, to make individuals aware of some of the costs and penalties of not being informed or taking action. Do not deem this chapter as gospel. Let it guide you, but do your own research. **When making important decisions, always consult an estate or trust attorney and a tax consultant. Remember, many retirement decisions are permanent—you get *NO DO-OVERS*.**

Revision, Revision, Revision

This chapter is proof of how fast laws change. In January 2020, the SECURE Act was approved by Congress and signed into law by President Donald Trump. Our original chapter, *Navigating the Retirement Account Labyrinth*, became instantly obsolete. The chapter had to be rewritten to address the many changes in the laws that apply to retirement accounts. Then the chapter had to be rewritten again with the enactment of the CARES Act.

CARES Act

President Trump signed the CARES Act into law on March 27, 2020. CARES is the acronym for the Coronavirus Aid, Relief, and Economic Security Act. The purpose of this act is to add stimulus money back into the economy to help businesses and individuals who have been financially impacted by the coronavirus.

The CARES Act suspends required minimum distributions (RMDs) for 2020 from retirement accounts, such as traditional IRAs, 401(k)s, and inherited accounts. This

means that for 2020 you do not have to withdraw an RMD from your retirement accounts. But by the time the law was passed, many individuals had already taken their required distributions.

So now what? On April 2, 2020, the Schwab Center for Financial Research published the article "Can You Forgo Taking RMDs in 2020?" which answers many questions and concerns related to RMDs and the CARES Act. You can find the article on Schwab's website.

Besides the changes for RMDs, the CARES Act includes many more aspects and law changes that may affect you personally. More changes and new laws are coming. Check the web and newspapers for updates.

SECURE Act

President Donald Trump signed the SECURE Act on December 20, 2019. This new set of laws took effect January 1, 2020. SECURE is an acronym for "Setting Every Community Up for Retirement Enhancement." Sounds simple. But the facts are the new laws within the SECURE Act are complex and require an understanding of the many changes to retirement accounts. As of the writing of this chapter, the SECURE Act is being evaluated by the media, accountants, and financial planners. They provide much speculation and interpretation as to what the SECURE Act laws really mean.

A limited amount of layperson information is shared in this chapter. But don't be surprised if the interpretations of the SECURE Act today will be different tomorrow. For details and guidance, seek professionals.

Traditional and Roth IRA Accounts

A **traditional** Individual Retirement Account **(traditional IRA)** and a **Roth** Individual Retirement Account **(Roth IRA)** are two different government retirement accounts, each with their own rules and regulations. The purpose of retirement accounts is to motivate taxpayers to put earned money from employment into saving plans while they are young and in the workforce.

To discourage account owners from spending money meant for retirement too soon, owners withdrawing funds before they reach the age of 59½ face a 10% tax penalty on their withdrawals. Some exceptions apply.

Traditional IRA RMDs

Earned money from an employer can be deposited into a traditional IRA savings account. No state or federal taxes are paid to the IRS for money invested or earned in the traditional IRA until the money is withdrawn. If invested wisely, traditional IRA accounts grow in value.

At a designated starting age, and then each year following, the IRS requires you to take a percentage of your saved funds out of your traditional IRA accounts and pay taxes on the withdrawn amount. The amount of money you are required to withdraw is known as a required minimum distribution (RMD). The IRS wants to start collecting money on any account you own that has been tax-deferred and allowed to grow for your retirement.

Calculating, Withdrawing, and Paying Taxes on RMDs

Once RMDs are started, the law requires an annual distribution thereafter by December 31 of each year. The total amount of your RMD can be withdrawn from any IRA account or a combination of those accounts.

Calculating, withdrawing, and paying taxes on RMDs is a two-year process. Here is how it works:

- Each year you will need to tell the institution(s) holding your tax-deferred account(s) the amount of money (RMD) to withdraw. Each year's required distribution will be different.
- Tell the institution the estimated percentage of federal and state taxes to withhold from your distribution—generally 25% federal and 10% state, depending on your income bracket. RMDs are taxed as ordinary income.
- The institution will distribute to you the amount of money you have requested to be withdrawn from your tax-deferred accounts minus the money you have requested to be paid for taxes owed.
- The institution then sends the money they withheld from your distribution to state and federal IRS services.

First year. Obtain the total value of all your prior year tax-deferred accounts. This would be the previous year's value on December 31, xxxx. Then refer to IRS Publication 590-B to determine the dollar amount (RMD) you must withdraw from your tax-deferred account(s). Use Appendix A and Appendix B in this publication to help you. Appendix A has a worksheet to help you determine the amount of RMD you are required to withdraw as well as providing a place to record a yearly history of your RMD withdrawals. Appendix B has Life Expectancy Tables. These tables show you the percentage of money (RMD) according to your age and tax status that you are required to withdraw. Multiply the percentage times the total value of your IRA accounts. The results are the amount

of money (RMD) you are required to withdraw from your retirement accounts and add as ordinary income on your state and federal tax returns. On any date during the year, instruct your IRA account holder to withdraw the requested RMD and to withhold and send required taxes to the state and federal IRS. After the deduction of taxes sent to the IRS, the institution will send you the dollar amount of the remaining RMD. It is best to complete this step early in the year so you do not forget.

Second year. The holder of your IRA account will send you Form 1099-R showing the amount of RMD withdrawn from your IRA account and the taxes they have paid to the IRS on your behalf. You should receive Form 1099-R by January 31 so you will be able to file this form with your April taxes. You will be able to use the money the institution has already paid the IRS as a tax credit on your tax returns.

Institutions often send clients a yearly statement advising how much RMD money needs to be withdrawn. With some financial institutions, account holders can arrange for the institution to calculate each year the amount you need to withdraw for your RMD. The institution will then automatically withdraw your RMD from your retirement account(s), withhold requested taxes, and send you the remaining money.

Ultimately, the Responsibility Is Yours

Essentially, the calculation, withdrawing, and payment of taxes on RMD accounts are your responsibility. Institutions have many accounts and variations of accounts to keep track of. Your account information and accountability could easily slip through the cracks. Never assume your request has been carried through. My husband recently called three times to follow up on a request to an institution regarding an RMD. Each call he talked to a different person and got three different answers.

The IRS sometimes waives penalties for mistakes made when making an RMD withdrawal by allowing 100% depletion of the IRA. Caveat: A 40% tax, or whatever tax bracket you are in, occurs on a traditional IRA withdrawn amount. The following table provides examples of taxes and penalties owed for an RMD done correctly, incorrectly, and ignored.

IRS Taxes and Penalties for RMD Withdrawals

CAUTION: Failure to withdraw an accurate yearly amount of money from a tax-deferred account when due results in a severe penalty.

Calculations

IRS Publication 590-B, Appendix B, Life Expectancy Tables

Example: Correct Withdrawal of RMD

$20,000 RMD required withdrawal (40% federal and state tax brackets)

RMD	$20,000
40% owed taxes	-8,000
Net in pocket	$12,000

Example: Failure to Withdraw RMD on Time

$20,000 RMD required withdrawal (40% federal and state tax brackets)

RMD	$20,000
40% owed taxes	-8,000
50% owed federal tax penalty	-10,000
Net in pocket	$2,000

Example: RMD Miscalculation

$20,000 RMD required withdrawal (40% federal & state tax brackets)

RMD withdrawal should have been	$20,000
Miscalculated and only withdrew	$12,000
RMD late withdrawal	$8,000
40% tax owed on $12,000	$4,800
40% tax owed on $8,000	3,200
50% owed federal tax penalty on $8,000 not withdrawn on time	4,000
Total taxes & penalties	$12,000
Net in pocket	$8,000

CARES Act—RMDs

As stated earlier, because of the CARES Act, no RMDs are required to be withdrawn from your retirement accounts for 2020. It is unknown at this point if this will be extended beyond 2020.

SECURE Act—RMDs

Now that the SECURE Act has been signed, owners of affected retirement accounts are not required to start taking RMDs until age 72; to qualify, a retirement account owner must have reached the age of 70½ after 2019. This allows one-and-a-half more years for tax-deferred accounts to grow in value without being depleted by distributions and taxes. This is a recognition that we are living longer and need more income to last to an older age.

Before January 1, 2020, owners of traditional IRA and retirement accounts had been required to begin taking RMDs from their accounts the year they reached 70½. Account owners who reached 70½ before and during 2019 will follow the laws established before the SECURE Act. Once RMDs are started, they must be continued.

If you turned 70½ in 2019, you were required to take an RMD for the 2019 tax year no later than April 1, 2020. You must have taken your second RMD, which was for the 2020 tax year, by December 31, 2020. If you have missed either RMD, you could face a 50% penalty on RMD funds that should have been withdrawn.

Roth IRA

Unlike traditional IRAs, you are required to pay taxes on earned income **before** putting money into a Roth account. Since taxes have been paid on your contributions, you can withdraw your contributions (money you put into a Roth account) at any time with no tax or penalty.

Five-Year Rule

Roth accounts must be open for five tax years before money **earned** on an original investment can be taken out tax-free and without a penalty.

Qualified Distribution Payment

An original Roth account owner, after fulfilling the five-year rule requirement and reaching the age of 59½, pays no taxes or penalties on contribution and earning distributions (profits) taken. **Any earnings (profits)** taken out of a Roth account before the five-year rule has been met are subject to taxes. If earnings are taken out before the five-year rule has been met and the owner has not reached the age of 59½, earnings are subject to taxes and a 10% penalty.

Listed below are qualified Roth IRA distributions that allow you to avoid paying taxes and the 10% early withdrawal penalty. To count as a qualified distribution, the payment **must meet both requirements**.

1. Distribution occurs at least five years after opening and funding the first Roth IRA.
2. Distribution is taken under one of these circumstances:
    a. You are at least 59½ years old.
    b. You have a disability.
    c. The payment is made to your beneficiary or to your estate after your death.
    d. The money is used to buy, build, or rebuild a home as a first-time homebuyer ($10,000 limit).
    e. A withdrawal of up to $5,000 is used toward the birth of a new child or adoption.

If you are not familiar with taxes and penalties you may face by making an unqualified distribution from your Roth IRA account, two examples are given.

Example 1: John

John (age 60) withdrew $8,000 from his Roth IRA. His original investment was $5,000, and his earnings were $3,000. John has not had the Roth IRA account for five years. Let's look at his situation (money was not in a Roth IRA for five years but the owner has reached age 59½) and how the rules apply. Roth IRA accounts must be open for five tax years before the money **earned** on an original investment can be withdrawn tax-free and without a penalty.

- Original Roth IRA stock investment with brokerage firm is $5,000.
- Roth IRA stock investment grows to $8,000.
- Original $5,000 contribution can be withdrawn tax-free.
- $3,000 is money earned and is taxable because John did not have the account for a total of five taxable years.

John owes state and federal income taxes on $3,000 of the $8,000 he withdrew.

Example 2: Tim

Tim (age 55) withdrew $8,000 from his Roth IRA. His original investment was $5,000, and his earnings were $3,000. He has had his Roth IRA for six years. Let's look at his situation and how the Roth IRA rule (money withdrawn from a Roth IRA before age 59½ is not a qualified distribution) applies.

- Original Roth IRA stock investment with brokerage firm was $5,000.
- Roth IRA stock investment grew to $8,000.
- Original $5,000 contribution can be withdrawn tax-free.
- $3,000 is money earned; $3,000 is taxable plus subject to a 10% federal tax penalty.

Tim owes state and federal income taxes on $3,000 of the $8,000 he withdrew, plus a 10% federal tax penalty of $300 because he took an unqualified distribution before age 59½.

Beneficiaries of Traditional and Roth IRA Retirement Accounts

Beneficiaries have various options available to manage an inherited retirement account. A few options have been included in this chapter to make you aware you do have choices. Consult a professional for advice on the correct choice to fit your situation.

The beneficiary or beneficiaries of an IRA account can be one person, multiple people, a trust, or a charity. The owner of an IRA can change a beneficiary at any time, but the change must be made in writing. If multiple beneficiaries are listed, identify the percentage of funds each beneficiary is to receive.

You should also name a contingent IRA beneficiary. A contingent beneficiary only receives money if the primary beneficiary disclaims beneficiary rights or dies before the IRA owner. More than one contingent beneficiary may be assigned.

If a deceased person's IRA has no designated beneficiary/beneficiaries, the representative in charge of the estate cashes out the IRA, allotting for approximately 25% federal and 10% state taxes owed.

IRA beneficiaries may be a son or daughter and are listed as *per stirpes.* If the son or daughter dies before the parent, and if the deceased has children, the children will receive the deceased son's or daughter's portion of the inherited IRA. When beneficiaries aren't designated as per stirpes, the IRA will be divided among the other beneficiaries and will not pass on to the next generations. Maya E. Dollarhide provides a good explanation of this process in Investopedia.

Upon the IRA owner's death, the beneficiaries are entitled to the IRA funds.

Beneficiary Forms

It is important to fill out all beneficiary forms for each retirement account correctly and to keep them updated with current information. When closing an estate, laws guiding the beneficiary of accounts will *first* follow beneficiary of retirement accounts instructions and then consideration of instructions set up in a will or trust.

Beneficiary forms are the most important guide to your wishes. Beneficiary forms correctly filled out and kept current will override a will or trust instructions 99% of the time. Follow these steps:

- Include full name of each beneficiary;
- Include beneficiary's Social Security number;
- Include percentage of fund beneficiary is to receive;
- Provide the beneficiary a copy of the information;
- At least once a year, update beneficiary forms;
- When birth, death, marriage, or divorce in a family occurs, fill out new forms;
- When an estate has more than one heir and the object is to divide assets equally, use the term "In Equal Shares";
- To confirm that the beneficiary's descendant(s) are part of the distribution of the estate, add *"per stirpes"* after the beneficiary's name and the percentage of entitlement;
- If the institution where money is held changes name or merges with another, fill out a new form (forms with old institution names often are not valid);
- Maintain hard copies of all beneficiary forms.

Life Lessons of Incorrect Beneficiary Forms

The importance of correctly identifying beneficiaries and keeping information current on retirement accounts is underestimated. There are many sad stories of what has happened to families when beneficiary forms have not been filled out properly.

In one such story, the deceased completed his beneficiary form by writing "To be distributed pursuant to my Last Will and Testament," thinking this statement would be sufficient for his children to receive the funds. As we have stated, the law only recognizes as legal a beneficiary form that specifies the name of each beneficiary along with the percentages of beneficiary funds designated by each name. The man's failure to fill out the beneficiary form correctly invalidated the document, making his wife of only two months the default beneficiary. The children fought in court to receive the $800,000 their dad had intended for them. Since his beneficiary form was invalid, the judge followed the rules of law, which made his new wife first in line to inherit his retirement funds.

Don't Be Me—My Husband's Hated Ex Inherited His Lucrative IRA

Let's look at another example of an inheritance gone wrong. John had left everything in his will to his current wife. His divorce from his first wife had been a long and bitter fight. His first wife was surprised and puzzled when she received $200,000 from her former husband's estate. Why? What happened? It wasn't intentional. John had neglected to change his IRA beneficiary form from his first wife to his current wife. It is incredible how often this happens. Ex-wife *ecstatic*; grieving widow *devastated*.

Inheritance Options

Uncle Joe, best uncle ever, just died and left you as his IRA beneficiary! You're all ready to cash out that inherited IRA and receive the money! Easy peasy! Or is it?

You actually have several choice selections, but there are also rules to follow. Many conditions are in play when deciding what to do with an inherited IRA.

Of course, a lump-sum distribution is an option. But is this wise? Closed retirement accounts no longer grow tax free, and you are likely to face a walloping tax bill.

Before making any decisions, consult a CPA, tax advisor, or elder attorney who specializes in IRAs. Consumers sometimes rely on bank employees or laypersons for advice. DON'T. They may not be aware of the rules or choices for your situation. If a mistake or wrong decision is made, you cannot go back and redo, and actions may result in strong financial penalties.

SECURE Act—Ten-Year Rule

The SECURE Act includes new tax laws for RMD withdrawals on IRAs. Effective January 1, 2020, retirement plans are guided by the ten-year rule for IRA accounts. RMDs for a majority of inherited traditional and Roth IRA accounts are no longer required, but a beneficiary for these accounts must completely withdraw all the account funds and close the account within ten years of the plan owner's death. For traditional IRA accounts, state and federal taxes are owed on withdrawn funds.

RMD rules for retirement accounts inherited from owners who died before 2020 are unchanged: a qualified IRA beneficiary was able to use the Life Expectancy Tables in IRS Publication 590-B and take RMDs over the beneficiary's lifetime using the beneficiary's age in place of the IRA owner's age.

Eligible Designated Beneficiary of a Traditional IRA

Of course, there are exceptions to the SECURE Act's ten-year rule. Heirs who meet the definition of "eligible designated beneficiary," a new term in the SECURE Act, are not subject to the ten-year rule. They are allowed to use their age and the Life Expectancy Tables in IRS Publication 590-B to calculate and take RMD withdrawals over their lifetime. An eligible designated beneficiary is limited to account owner's surviving spouse, his/her minor child, a beneficiary who is no more than ten years younger than the account owner, or a chronically ill individual.

Following is an example of one of the interpretations of a child inheriting a parent's IRA. This interpretation could change over time.

> An eleven-year-old child's parents have died and left the child an inherited IRA. The child lives in California where the majority age is eighteen. The child is required to have minimum distributions taken out of the inherited account based on his/her age and the Life Expectancy Tables in IRS Publication 590-B until the child reaches majority age, which is eighteen in California. At age eighteen, the child has ten years to withdraw the remainder of the inherited account. After age eighteen, no more minimum distributions are required, but the account must be emptied of funds by the time the child reaches age twenty-eight.

It is important to note the age of majority (the age that a person is considered a legal adult is different depending on what state you live in). In every state except Nebraska, Alabama, and Mississippi, the age of majority is eighteen. In Nebraska and Alabama, the majority age is nineteen, and in Mississippi, it is twenty-one.

Spousal Inherited Traditional IRA

The rules are somewhat different for spouses who inherit traditional IRAs. A surviving spouse is the **only** exception to the rule of **never changing an inherited IRA into your own name.** A surviving spouse has a spousal rollover option of his/her deceased spouse's IRA. He/she can roll over all or part of the IRA into his/her own IRA. This is a good option if the surviving spouse doesn't need the funds, and an RMD is not yet required because of the surviving spouse's younger age. Making the rollover into the spouse's name now allows the spouse to take out RMDs based on his/her own life expectancy. A rollover must be completed within sixty days of receiving distribution. The distribution cannot contain RMD funds. Request "spousal rollover" forms to make the change. Once the IRA is rolled over, the surviving spouse must be 59½ to make withdrawals without a 10% penalty. Remember to set up beneficiaries for the rolled-over IRA.

If the spouse is not the sole beneficiary of the IRA account, the spouse's portion of the inherited IRA is allowed to be transferred into an IRA that has been set up and

named as an inherited IRA. Be aware that no additional contributions are allowed in the inherited IRA account.

If the deceased spouse had not reached the age that he/she would have been required to take RMDs, the surviving spouse has the option to completely withdraw IRA funds within five years, and even if he/she is not yet 59½ will not receive a penalty for an early withdrawal.

Disclaim/Decline to Inherit Disclaimer

A beneficiary can *refuse* to inherit an IRA for any reason. This is called "disclaiming" the benefits, and the *refusal* is called a *disclaimer*. Following are the rules that govern a disclaimer:

- A beneficiary of an IRA can choose not to inherit IRA assets and disclaim the benefits to the next generation. When this option is chosen, the IRA assets pass to the deceased owner's contingent beneficiaries. Contingent beneficiaries could be children, grandchildren, another relative, a trust, or a charity.
- The beneficiary must provide an irrevocable and unqualified refusal to accept the assets.
- The refusal must be in writing.
- The beneficiary must not have accepted any of the inherited assets prior to the disclaimer.
- Assets must pass to the successor beneficiary without any direction on the part of the person making the disclaimer.
- If the inherited IRA is passed on to a minor child of the deceased, the child must take RMD withdrawals on his/her Life Expectancy Tables in IRS Publication 590-B until the minor child reaches the age of majority. Once the child reaches the age of majority, the ten-year rule applies.
- An IRA passed as an inherited IRA to another beneficiary, other than a minor child of the deceased, must immediately follow the ten-year rule.
- *The election to disclaim IRA assets is irrevocable.* This option must be taken within nine months of an owner's death. Make sure to seek professional advice before making any decisions.

Titling the Transfer of an IRA Account to a Beneficiary

It is critical that non-spousal-inherited IRAs be correctly titled when transferred to a beneficiary. DO NOT change an inherited IRA to your name or allow a custodian to do so. Request that the institution holding the IRA change the inherited IRA title from "inheritor by a trustee" to "trustee transfer." A name change sets in motion a legally required distribution of all the IRA assets and closes the IRA. Funds, intentionally or unintentionally, are then no longer part of an IRA and can't be ever again. All the funds in the IRA are required to be withdrawn, taxes paid on withdrawn funds, and the account closed.

Titling an inherited IRA requires three items:
- name of the owner (the person who died),
- the word "IRA," and
- the statement "it is for the benefit of the heir."

Here's an example:

John Doe IRA (Deceased January 1, 2020)

For Benefit of Jane Doe, Inherited IRA Benefiicary

Rules on **how to**, **timing,** and **naming** of account transfers are very strict, and if not exactly followed, an IRA can be dissolved. Check with the account holder to make sure all rules are followed correctly. Mistakes may result in catastrophic consequences that can never be undone.

Roth Beneficiaries

A surviving spouse who is the sole beneficiary of a deceased spouse's Roth IRA is eligible to do a Roth IRA spousal rollover and treat the Roth IRA as his/her own. The spouse isn't required to withdraw any distributions in his/her lifetime. A surviving spouse must name a new beneficiary/beneficiaries for a rolled-over or transferred IRA account.

A spouse and non-spouse beneficiary of a Roth IRA account is allowed to withdraw Roth IRA **contributions** tax free any time. But to avoid paying taxes on **earnings**, the beneficiary must be sure the Roth IRA has been open for five years.

Like a traditional IRA, all funds for non-spouse beneficiaries must be withdrawn within ten years.

Deceased Person's IRA

IRA name	Holder name	Account number	Contact telephone	Value at date of death	Web address	Password

Beneficiary of Deceased Person's IRA

Beneficiary	% of Fund	Relationship	Social Security #	Notes

Simplified Checklist of Transactions of IRA Accounts, Non-Spousal

✓

	Get the account numbers and passwords needed to access the account(s).
	The IRA holder, while still alive, gives each beneficiary of the IRA a letter with the name, address, phone number, and account number of the institution holding the IRA.
	The IRA holder gives each inheritor a copy of the beneficiary form.
	When the IRA holder passes away, each heir should obtain, depending on the required information, an original or copy of the death certificate to proceed.
	Each beneficiary should contact the institution holding the IRA account and discuss the proper paperwork needed for his/her purpose and situation. Each heir should request that the transition paperwork be emailed or mailed to him/her. The form may be identified as IRA Beneficiary Transfer/Distribution Form, IRA Beneficiary Claim Form, or IRA Inheritance Form.
	Have the institution holding the IRA correctly add the title "Inherited IRA" to the inheritor's name. For example: John Doe IRA (Deceased January 1, 2019) For Benefit of Jim Doe, Inherited IRA Beneficiary
	Change the Social Security number on each account to the new holder.
	The individual in charge of closing the estate is responsible for the RMD withdrawal until the IRA is closed or transferred. If not done correctly, the estate faces a 50% penalty on the RMD amount that should have been taken.
	The individual in charge of closing the estate is responsible for informing the beneficiaries if the deceased was currently taking RMDs on IRA accounts, if the individual in charge of closing the estate started taking RMDs, and the date and amount of the RMDs taken.
	Fill out new beneficiary forms for the inherited IRA naming the new beneficiary or beneficiaries.
	Fill out new IRA contingent beneficiary/beneficiaries form(s).

IRA Accounts Owned by Surviving Spouse

IRA name	Holder name	Account number	Contact telephone	Value at date of death	Web address	Password

Surviving Spouse IRA Beneficiaries

Beneficiary	% of Fund	Relationship	Social Security #	Notes

Simplified Transactions for
Surviving Spouse IRA Accounts Checklist

✓

	If the deceased spouse was a "primary beneficiary," remove the deceased's name on the beneficiary form.
	To change the beneficiary/beneficiaries, call the IRA holder and request applicable forms or download forms from the web.
	File a new beneficiary form with the IRA administrator.
	Use the information in this chapter to determine how to properly fill out new beneficiary forms for the inherited IRA.

Workplace Retirement Accounts

401(k) and 403(b) Tax-Deferred Accounts

401(k)s and 403(b)s are tax-deferred accounts originating from your employer. Many workplace saving plans' rules are not uniform, as rules and investment options are set and administered by the employer offering the plan. The IRS sets the outside limits of what plans may do, but a plan is allowed to be more restrictive than that general framework. For example, the IRS may say it is OK to leave an account for years without touching it or paying taxes, but an employee plan rules may stipulate money must be taken out sooner.

When a person retires or is no longer working for the company where a 401(k) or 403(b) account was acquired, some employers may let the account continue while other employers may request an account of $5,000 or less be terminated. You can then choose to close the account or transfer to an IRA. Closing the account can lead to taxes and penalties, so seek advice from a tax or retirement expert.

Exceptions to Penalty for Early Withdrawal

If you are fifty-five or older at the time you stop working for a company, even if you quit, you can cash out your employee savings plan, penalty-free, under the "separation from service" exception. Taxes owed on an account must be paid. Other exceptions apply in cases of:

- permanent disability,
- unreimbursed medical expenses exceeding 10% of adjusted gross income,
- an election to receive "equal periodic payments" lasting for at least five years or until age 59½,
- the account holder dies and funds are distributed to the beneficiaries,

- a qualified military reservist called to active duty, or
- a court order to surrender the funds to an ex-spouse or dependent.

RMD Rules and Guidelines

A 401(k) retirement account is required to comply with the SECURE Act laws for RMDs:

1) allowing you to wait until age 72 to take RMDs if you haven't reached the age of 70½ before January 1, 2020;
2) governing inheritance of spouse and non-spouse accounts.

If you have a 403(b) or 457 retirement plan for government workers or a Thrift Savings Plan for federal employees, you have an additional two years to comply with the new SECURE Act laws, meaning if you inherit one of these accounts from a deceased individual **before January 1, 2022**, you can follow old rules and choose to take RMDs and associated tax payments over your lifetime.

Working at Age 72 and Beyond

If you are still working at age seventy-two and enrolled in an employee retirement plan, you are allowed to keep making contributions to the plan as long as you are not a 5% company owner. Also, you are not required to start withdrawing RMDs from an employee plan until you retire.

Inheriting from 401(k) and 403(b) Accounts

At death, 401(k) and 403(b) accounts become property of the beneficiary, and distributions are taxed based on the relationship to the deceased. If you are the beneficiary of a 401(k) or 403(b) plan, consult a tax professional to help determine options available for receiving the money and income tax consequences of the different options.

For California and other community property states, money earned while married and put into 401(k) and 403(b) accounts technically belongs to both the husband and wife. Therefore by law, the spouse is the required beneficiary of the account. To name a beneficiary other than your spouse, both spouses must agree and sign a waiver.

If an employee dies before retiring, the account goes directly to the beneficiary/beneficiaries. If there are no designated beneficiaries, the account moves to the estate of the deceased.

Use the following worksheets to help keep track of accounts and beneficiaries, and to see at a glance what steps need to be taken by a surviving spouse.

401(k), 403(b) Accounts Owned By Deceased

Account(s)	Holder name	Account number	Contact telephone	Value at date of death	Web address	Password

Deceased Account Beneficiaries

Beneficiary	% of Fund	Relationship	Social Security #	Notes

Simplified Checklist of Transactions for 401(k) or 403(b) Accounts

Guidelines for Surviving Spouse

✓	
	Get account number(s), password(s), and user names needed to access account(s).
	Depending on the employer's plan rules, a surviving spouse who is the sole beneficiary usually has the following choices: • Leave funds in the existing account until the year the deceased spouse would have been 72. • Roll over into the surviving spouse's employer-sponsored plan. RMD begins when the heir turns 72. • Do a spousal rollover into an IRA, changing the accounts to the survivor's name. • Change to an inherited IRA.
	Obtain an original or copy of the death certificate for each 401(k) or 403(b) account.
	Ask the account holder if an original or copy of the death certificate is required to proceed.
	Set up new beneficiary/beneficiaries, using information discussed earlier in this chapter. If the surviving spouse does not designate a beneficiary, typically the account would become part of the estate.

401(k), 403(b) Accounts Owned by Surviving Spouse

Account(s)	Holder name	Account number	Contact telephone	Value at date of death	Web address	Password

Surviving Spouse Account Beneficiaries

Beneficiary	% of Fund	Relationship	Social Security #	Notes

CHAPTER 7

The Medicare,
Medigap Maze

The most important information you need to remember about Medicare and Medigap plans is that rules and regulations change rapidly and rates differ year to year. In order to keep up with the most current information, know your best bet is to monitor updates on *official* US government websites—don't get fooled by the "look-alike" sites that are trying to sell you something or steal your personal information.

< Official US website: www.Medicare.gov. >

You can find information, apply for coverage, learn about costs, download publications, and much more. If you prefer to speak to someone on the phone, call 1-800-Medicare or 1-800-633-4227. The Medicare website states beneficiaries may call for help with their coverage, claims, payments and more. Help is available in English and Spanish, 24 hours a day, 7 days per week.

< Equally important is the official Social Security website: SocialSecurity.gov. **>**

If you need more information after visiting the website and need to speak to a Social Security representative, you may call 1-800-772-1213, Monday through Friday, from 8 a.m. to 5:30 p.m.

NEVER talk to a Social Security or Medicare "agent" who calls you unexpectedly without verifying their identity. Official government agencies do not make calls demanding payment or looking for information. If you receive a call, do NOT give out your Social Security or Medicare number or any other personal information. If you think it might be a valid call, hang up and call the authenticated Social Security phone number to make sure you are actually talking to a legitimate employee.

The following pages include various key enrollment information and additional data for Medicare and Medigap plans.

Who Gets Medicare?

At age sixty-five you are magically entitled to a Medicare plan. True or false?

As with everything government-related, it is complicated. Required qualifications include the following, but different rules and standards apply to distinct situations.

Qualifications for US Citizens Age 65 and Over

A US citizen is eligible for Medicare Part A, Part B, Part C, Part D, and Medigap at the age of sixty-five.

Noncitizens can purchase Medicare Part B if they:

- are legally admitted to the United States,
- are a legal resident for five consecutive years prior to applying for Medicare,
- have legal status at the moment of application.

A noncitizen who is entitled to purchase Medicare Part B can also purchase Medicare Part D.

Qualifications for US Citizens Under Age 65

Individuals under age sixty-five may qualify to receive Medicare if they:

- are receiving Social Security disability benefits and have received them for 24 months (two-year waiting period);
- receive Social Security disability because of amyotrophic lateral sclerosis (ALS), also known as Lou Gehrig's disease, or end stage renal disease (ESRD), also known as permanent kidney failure, and need dialysis. There is no waiting interval for either disease.

Because Social Security and Medicare eligibility rules are complex, it is recommended that you call Social Security at 1-800-772-1213 to get the most accurate information regarding your situation.

Is Enrollment Automatic?

Some individuals make the choice to receive reduced Social Security benefits as early as age sixty-two. In this case, look for a "Welcome to Medicare" packet from Medicare three months before turning sixty-five. Other important deadlines and actions need to be taken, so it is necessary to carefully read all provided materials.

If you are receiving Social Security benefits when you turn sixty-five and are eligible, the Social Security Administration automatically signs you up for Medicare Part A and Part B.

If you're not receiving Social Security benefits when you turn sixty-five, you won't get Medicare automatically, so you need to enroll in Medicare Part A (hospital insurance) and Part B (medical insurance). Sign up for Medicare online at Medicare.gov, or contact Social Security, where a representative can review your records to see if you qualify.

A Medicare recipient is able to select insurance from:

- Medicare Parts A and B, funded by the US government.
- Medicare Part C, Medicare Advantage Plans available through private health insurance companies.
- Medicare Part D, prescription drug coverage. Medicare Part C and Part D enrollment is only allowed with an insurance company in your zip code.
- Medigap plans are provided by private health insurance companies and can be viewed at Medicare.gov.

Medicare Initial Enrollment Period and Penalties

Timing is essential. Enroll in Medicare as soon as you are eligible to get the best coverage and avoid penalties. Your **initial** Medicare open enrollment period stretches seven months:

- beginning three months before the month you turn sixty-five,
- including the month you turn sixty-five,
- ending three months after the month you turn sixty-five.

The advantages to enrolling during your allowed time period are insurance companies:

- cannot request a health physical.
- cannot decline to insure you.

The disadvantages of enrolling outside your allowed time period are insurance companies:

- have the authority to request a health physical.
- may decline to insure you.

Medicare Part A
(Hospital Insurance)

Medicare recipients generally don't pay any premiums out of pocket for Medicare Part A. This is known as *premium-free Part A*. To qualify for *premium-free Part A*, you must have earned forty credits by paying taxes into the Federal Insurance Contributions Act (FICA). FICA is a tax withheld from your salary or self-employment income that funds the Social Security and Medicare programs. A person lacking credits may be required to pay a Medicare Part A premium. When lacking the forty credits, your monthly premium could be as high as $471 (for 2021). The more credits earned by paying into FICA, the more this dollar amount is reduced.

If you don't enroll in Part A when you're first eligible, your monthly premiums could go up 10%. You would pay your monthly premium plus an additional charge of 10% for two times the number of years you were eligible to sign up for Part A but didn't. A two-year delay in enrolling in Part A could raise the cost of your monthly premiums by 10% for four years.

If you enroll in Part A, you are also required to enroll in Part B.

Medicare Part B
(Medical Insurance)

Part B is medical insurance that helps pay for preventive services, durable medical equipment, and medical transportation. It also covers physicians' services, including those provided by doctors, surgeons, and anesthetists in the hospital or a skilled-nursing facility, or as part of home healthcare or hospice benefits.

Medicare Part B also covers healthcare received in the hospital if you are there "under observation" and **not as an officially admitted inpatient**, even if you are in a hospital bed and receiving the same kind of care as any other patient. In this situation, your care is covered under Medicare B, not A.

If you are enrolled in Medicare Part B, your monthly premium will automatically be deducted from your Social Security entitlement. The standard premium starts at $148.50 (for 2021). Social Security figures your premium amount based on your IRS tax return filed two years prior. For the year 2021, if your adjusted gross income was $88,000 or greater (single or married filing separately) or $176,000 (married filing jointly), your premium will cost more. This additional cost is referred to as an Income-Related Monthly Adjustment Amount (IRMAA).

A patient's **yearly** deductible for services is $203.00 (for 2021). After a patient pays a yearly deductible, Medicare pays 80% of Medicare B-approved medical costs, and the patient is responsible for the remaining 20%.

If you were eligible and enrolled late, you will incur a penalty. This could result in a possible permanent 10% monthly premium increase for each 12-month period you were eligible and did not enroll. Waiting three years to enroll could mean a 30% increase on your initial monthly premium. The 30% increase added to the initial monthly premium will be your new **lifetime** monthly premium.

Medicare Part C
(Medicare Advantage Plans)

Medicare Parts A, B, and D work together. Medicare Part C is its own entity. It doesn't follow the rules and regulations of Medicare Parts A, B, and D. Therefore, Medicare Part C is discussed later in this chapter.

Medicare Part D
(Prescription Drug Coverage)

Prescription drug plans are offered by many companies to the public. Each plan covers a variety of drugs. The monthly premium each plan charges depends on what type of prescription drugs the plan offers and how expensive the covered drugs are. Investigate and choose a plan that fits your needs. Different rules apply to people who are considered low-income or who qualify for state or government assistance.

Purchasers of Medicare Parts A and B are required to purchase Medicare Part D as soon as they are eligible unless they have other creditable prescription drug coverage. Failure to comply with this timeline results in a penalty.

If you are eligible for Medicare, are not covered by a prescription drug plan, and do not enroll in a plan during the initial enrollment period, you may face a possible added 1% increase to your monthly premium, times the number of months (rounded to the nearest $0.10) you were late. After you join a Medicare drug plan, the plan will tell you if you owe a penalty and what your premium will be. In most cases, you will be required to pay the penalty as long as you are enrolled in Medicare Part D.

Medicare calculates the penalty by multiplying 1% of the "national base beneficiary premium" $33.06 (for 2021) by the number of full, uncovered months you didn't have Part D or creditable coverage. The monthly premium is rounded to the nearest $0.10 and added to your monthly Part D premium.

The national base beneficiary premium may change each year, so your penalty amount may also change.

Penalty for late enrollment in Medicare Part D is confusing. Here is an example from the 2020 Medicare booklet.

> Mrs. Martinez had been eligible for Medicare during her initial enrollment period ending on May 31, 2016. She didn't have prescription drug coverage from any other source and waited to join Medicare Part D during the open enrollment period ending December 7, 2018. Her drug coverage became effective January 1, 2019.
>
> **2019 Premium.** Since Mrs. Martinez was without creditable prescription drug coverage from June 2016 through December 2018, her penalty in 2019 was 31% (1% for each of the 31 months) of $33.19 (the national base beneficiary premium for 2019), or $10.29. Since the monthly penalty is always rounded to the nearest $0.10, she was required to pay $10.30 each month **in addition** to her plan's monthly premium.
>
> **2020 Premium.** Medicare recalculated Mrs. Martinez's penalty using the 2020 base beneficiary premium of $32.74. Mrs. Martinez's new monthly penalty in 2020 is 31% of $32.74, or $10.15 each month. Since the monthly penalty is always rounded to the nearest $0.10, she pays $10.20 each month **in addition** to her plan's monthly premium.

The Medicare Income-Related Monthly Adjustment Amount (IRMAA)

Betty and John were set. They had been enrolled in Medicare Part B and Part D for five years. They enrolled on time and avoided any penalties. One day they received a notice from the Social Security Administration (SSA). Betty's Medicare Part B premium was going up $231.40 per month. John's Medicare Part B premium was going up $231.40 per month. What? Not possible?

John and Betty are both retired and a couple of years ago decided to take a dream vacation cruise and do needed home repairs. They withdrew a total of $100,000 out of John's traditional IRA account. When they filed their income tax for 2018, their joint filing income went from $174,000 to $274,000. In January 2020, the SSA notified them their monthly premiums for Medicare Part B and Part D now included an IRMAA—a surcharge. Like magic, each month $376 was automatically deducted from John's Social Security benefit and $376 from Betty's. Also, an additional monthly premium payment (IRMAA) of $50.70 for each was added to the amount they were already paying for Medicare Part D. Since Betty and John's income adjusted back down in 2019, their Medicare Part B premiums will adjust back to the lesser amount, and a Medicare Part D surcharge will no longer be applicable in 2021.

The Medicare IRMAA for Medicare Part B went into effect in 2007, and the IRMAA for Part D was implemented in 2011 as part of the Affordable Care Act. Again, this illustrates how important it is to know when, if, and how much RMDs to withdraw from your retirement accounts. Remember Social Security looks back two years on your taxes for an increase in your taxable income, so be aware and don't be caught off guard. If you filed jointly with a spouse, Social Security will base your premiums for each of you based on that married income. However, you will EACH pay your own Part B and Part D premiums. Your premiums are always individual, not combined. Social Security simply uses your household income to determine where you fall individually in the premiums chart. A chart has been included for your own calculations.

Medicare Part B Premiums and Part D IRMAA—Year 2021

Based Upon 2019 Income

Important Note: (1) Income tax brackets for a required IRMAA, (2) the cost of Medicare Part B premiums, and (3) Part D IRMAA monthly premiums are subject to change every year.

Income brackets as filed on income tax return	Medicare Part B monthly premium per income	Medicare Part D IRMAA increased $$$ amount added to your monthly premium
Single		
$88,000 or less	$148.50	-0-
$88,001 up to $111,000	$207.90	+$12.30
$111,001 up to $138,000	$297.00	+$31.80
$138,001 up to $165,000	$386.10	+$51.20
$165,001 less than $500,000	$475.20	+$70.70

(Continued)

Income brackets as filed on income tax return.	Medicare Part B monthly premium per income.	Medicare Part D IRMAA increased $$$ amount added to your monthly premium.
$500,000 and above	$504.90	+$77.10

Married Filing Jointly

Income brackets as filed on income tax return.	Medicare Part B monthly premium per income.	Medicare Part D IRMAA increased $$$ amount added to your monthly premium.
$176,000 or less	$148.50	-0-
$176,001 up to $222,000	$207.90	+$12.30
$222,001 up to $276,000	$297.00	+$31.80
$276,001 up to $330,000	$386.10	+$51.20
$330,001 and less than $750,000	$475.20	+$70.70
$750,00 and above	$504.90	+$77.10

Married Filing Separately

Income brackets as filed on income tax return.	Medicare Part B monthly premium per income.	Medicare Part D IRMAA increased $$$ amount added to your monthly premium.
$88,000 or less	$148.50	-0-
$88,001 and less than $412,000	$475.20	+$70.70
$412,000 and above	$504.90	+$77.10

Medicare Coverage for Hospital and Skilled Nursing

Details in this section are provided to make you aware of your options and to help you understand the fundamentals of hospital and skilled-nursing Medicare coverage. The rules that follow are complicated and not easily understood. Each year premiums and deductibles change. Do your own investigation before using this information.

Billing Definitions

- **Coinsurance** is an amount you may be required to pay as your share of the cost for services after you pay any deductibles. Coinsurance is usually a percentage, for example 20%.
- **Insurance deductible** is the amount of money you will pay for an insurance claim before coverage kicks in and the insurance company starts paying.
- **Copayment** is an amount required to be paid as your share of the cost for a medical service or supply, like a doctor or hospital outpatient visit, or prescription drug.

A copayment is usually a set amount, rather than a percentage. For example, you might pay $10 or $20 for each doctor's visit or prescription drug.

Benefit Period

Original Medicare Part A combines a timeline for a patient's hospital and skilled-nursing facility inpatient care known as a benefit period. A benefit period is the way original Medicare Part A measures the number of days you have spent as an inpatient in a hospital and skilled-nursing facility. **It begins the first day you are registered as an inpatient at a hospital and ends when you have not received Medicare-covered inpatient-hospital or skilled-nursing facility (SNF) care for sixty consecutive days.** After not receiving either Medicare-covered hospital and SNF inpatient care for sixty consecutive days, you are eligible to begin a new benefit period. There is no limit to the number of benefit periods you are entitled to.

A Medicare Part A patient is eligible for full and partial Medicare-paid hospital coverage for ninety days and healthcare nursing facility coverage for one hundred days per one benefit period.

A doctor must give an official order stating inpatient care is needed to treat an illness or an injury. An individual is allowed to be discharged and readmitted to a hospital or skilled-nursing facility several times during a benefit period for the same doctor-diagnosed injury or illness. The readmittance to a facility must be within a reasonable length of time as determined by Medicare. Variations of plans covered under Medicare C (PPO, HMO, and Kaiser) follow different guidelines.

The admittance to a nursing home must (1) coincide within thirty days of a hospitalization and (2) be for the same or a related condition that caused the hospitalization. Qualifying expenses may include a semiprivate room, meals, skilled nursing, rehabilitative services, medical social services, and limited transportation. Medicare Part B covers partial expenses incurred for physician services that are provided by doctors, surgeons, and anesthetists.

Medicare Part A Hospital Cost—90 Days Allowed for One Benefit Period

Each benefit period a patient is responsible for paying a $1,484 deductible (for 2021) the first day he/she is admitted to a hospital. After the patient pays the deductible payment, Medicare pays hospital costs for days one through sixty. Days sixty-one through ninety, the patient pays $371 (for 2021) in coinsurance per day, and Medicare pays the patient's hospital costs above $371 (for 2021).

Skilled-Nursing Facility Cost
100 Days Allowed for One Benefit Period

A patient is eligible for expenses to be paid by Medicare to a skilled-nursing facility after a three-day minimum medically necessary **inpatient** hospital stay.

Medicare pays the nursing-facility costs for the first twenty days, and the patient coinsurance is zero. If a patient needs further care beyond twenty days, the patient is responsible to cover coinsurance costs of $185.50 per day (for 2021) for days twenty-one through one hundred. The length of stay beyond one hundred days is fully at the expense of the patient. An inpatient hospital stay begins the day the hospital admits a patient and does not include the day of discharge. To qualify for care in a skilled-nursing facility, a doctor must certify a need for daily skilled care, such as intravenous injections or physical therapy.

Additional Optional Hospital Days Allowed Coverage

If you use all your allowed benefit days of coverage during one benefit period, you still have a couple of options. After a ninety-day hospital stay in one benefit period, if needed, a patient has the option of using a "lifetime sixty-day reserve" to help pay hospital costs. A patient using these reserve days will pay a $742 (for 2021) daily copay for each day used of the sixty allowed. **Once the sixty days are used, they are gone forever.**

Patients who own Medigap policies A through N are provided an additional 365 lifetime reserve days of 100% coverage for Medicare Part A coinsurance and hospital costs.

Some of the costs for hospital and skilled-nursing facilities have been explained, but also consider that your personal items are not covered. So, avoid surprises, ask questions, and become informed BEFORE you get your bill! The following charts may be helpful.

Medicare Part A Hospital Stay
One Benefit Period
Patient responsibility may be fully or partially paid by Medigap plans, when applicable.
Costs quoted are for year 2021 coverage.

Length of stay	Patient responsibility	Medicare pays
Days 1–60	First day $1,484 (Part A deductible)	Hospital costs above $1,484
Days 61–90	$371 per day coinsurance 29 days x $371 = $10,759	Hospital costs above $371/day

If a patient needs to stay in the hospital longer during a benefit period, he/she may use a portion or all of the optional "lifetime sixty-day reserve." However, BEWARE: Once days are used, they are gone forever.

"lifetime sixty-day reserve" Days 91–150	$742 daily coinsurance $742 per day x 60 = $44,520	Hospital costs above $742/day

Medicare Part A Skilled Nursing
One Benefit Period
Medicare skilled nursing coincides with a hospital stay benefit period. Coinsurance may be fully or partially covered by Medigap plans, when applicable.

Skilled nursing one benefit period	Patient responsibility
Days 1–20	Zero for all approved amounts
Days 21–100	Coinsurance $185.50 per day (for 2021)
Days beyond 100	All expenses

Medigap—365 Lifetime-Reserve Days

Medigap policyholders have an additional 365 lifetime-reserve days of 100% coinsurance and hospital costs coverage after Medicare's sixty lifetime-reserve days have been used up. You may use a few or all additional lifetime-reserve days for a hospital stay. **Once the 365 days have been used, they are gone forever.**

Lucy Received a "MOON"

Lucy's story will demonstrate some of the complexities of Medicare hospital and skilled-nursing coverage.

The knife blade sliced deep into Lucy's hand while she was fixing supper. Lucy had just had her knife set sharpened as she had been told several times there was less chance of an accident with a sharp knife. *Yeah, right! Ouch.* Blood everywhere! Lucy was in so much pain, she knew she had no way to escape a hospital visit.

At the hospital, she learned the wound needed extensive surgical repair and a skin graft. The surgery completed, Lucy was in a hurry to check out of the hospital and return home, and she did just that against her doctor's advice. Her doctor had advised her to spend another day in the hospital and recommended skilled-nursing care in a facility that would provide daily care for her and her wound. At Lucy's insistence, she was discharged on the fourth day of her stay and told her wound would heal slowly because she was elderly.

Once home, she discovered that her surgery had left her with little energy, and she was not competent to properly clean and dress her wound. What was she thinking? She could not make a meal for herself or wash dishes. She called her doctor and told him he was right, and it was a good idea that she recuperate in a nursing facility.

But Lucy discovered her Medicare plan would not pay for her nursing-facility care, and here is why. Her first day in the hospital had been charted as "patient observation." Medicare's three-day rule required her to be an admitted hospital patient for three consecutive days, not counting the day of discharge, before they would pay any skilled-nursing facility expenses. She had only been an inpatient for two days.

She confronted the hospital and asked why she had been in their facility for three days but did not qualify through Medicare to go into a skilled-nursing facility for needed care. The hospital was quick to explain that she had received "MOON" paperwork, Medicare Outpatient Observation Notice, with her discharge papers. The MOON paperwork noted her first day had been only as an outpatient for observation. They were sorry Lucy did not understand Medicare's three-day rule.

Know the significance of an action. Be aware Lucy was anxious to return home, but her option of twenty days of Medicare-paid skilled-nursing care to help her heal and rest was closed to her because she was ignorant of the consequences of her choice.

Medicare Part C
(Medicare Advantage Plans)

Medicare Part C is made up of insurance plans that replace regular Medicare Parts A, B, and D. Medicare Part C is a separate category with different rules and copays depending on your plan. They can be preferred provider organizations (PPOs) or health maintenance organizations (HMOs). Kaiser Permanente Senior Advantage plan is one example of a Medicare Part C plan. In these plans, Medicare Parts A and B are combined into one plan. Some Medicare Advantage plans also include prescription drug coverage as well as vision and dental care. These plans often offer a limited selection of doctors and hospitals.

Preferred Provider Organization (PPO)

You sign up to be a member of a PPO network and pay less when you use doctors, hospitals, and other healthcare providers belonging to your PPO network. You will pay more to use providers and services outside the network.

Health Maintenance Organization (HMO)

An HMO is an organized public or private entity that provides basic and supplemental health services to its subscribers. The organization secures its network of health providers by entering into contracts with primary care physicians, clinical facilities, and specialists. The medical entities that enter into contracts with the HMO are paid an agreed fee to offer a range of services to subscribers. An HMO typically offers lower premiums than other types of insurance plans. Be aware that a patient using a doctor or health facility out of the HMO network may not get any insurance coverage for those services. HMOs may offer prescription drug coverage as well.

Kaiser Permanente Senior Advantage

Kaiser Permanente is an HMO operating in California and a limited number of other states. Be aware that some areas of the United States do NOT have Kaiser doctors or facilities. Even in California, you will find some cities have Kaiser doctors and facilities while other cities do not. If you move away from a Kaiser service area, you may find it difficult to get a comparable plan.

Kaiser has its own network of doctors, hospitals, and pharmacies and offer plans with different monthly premiums and deductibles for items and services. Group members must also consider that Kaiser benefits, premiums, copayments, and coinsurance may change on January 1 of each year or other times according to contracts.

Summary of Various Medicare Plans

Specific medical plans pay a percentage of consumer costs for products and services. Each plan has specified time periods, restrictions, and exceptions for paying patients' claims.

Medicare Part A	Inpatient hospital care Skilled-nursing facility Hospice Home healthcare
Medicare Part B	Services from doctors and other healthcare providers Hospital outpatient care Durable medical equipment and home healthcare Medical transportation Preventive services Health maintenance, prevents illnesses from getting worse
Medicare Part C	Healthcare through provider organizations like HMOs and PPOs Costs vary, with some plans requiring no monthly premiums Includes all benefits, services covered under Parts A and B Run by Medicare-approved private insurance companies Usually includes prescription drug coverage May include extra benefits and services for an extra cost
Medicare Part D	Prescription drug coverage Coverage provided by Medicare-approved private insurance companies Prescription drug coverage required to enroll in Medigap plans
Medigap Supplemental	Supplemental insurance sold by private companies May not enroll in a Medigap plan if enrolled in a Medicare Advantage, Medicare Part C plan

Medigap Plans

Medigap has a one-time, six-month open enrollment period, one month less than Medicare. This six-month period automatically starts the month you turn sixty-five, and **once you miss open enrollment, you have missed it forever.** To enroll in Medigap, you must first enroll in Medicare Part A and B.

Medigap plans are supplemental private insurance plans sold in most states. Each state has its own Medigap plans and guidelines. Medigap helps pay the deductibles, copays, and coinsurance payments for Medicare Parts A and B patients.

During **Medigap open enrollment**, an insurance company can't deny a Medicare supplemental policy or charge a higher premium because of preexisting conditions. A supplemental plan can be purchased regardless of any preexisting health conditions.

Of course, to baffle you, California also provides an annual open enrollment to add, disenroll, or change Medigap policies. Do not confuse this with the one-time Medigap open enrollment that is allowed when you turn sixty-five.

Something to Consider

If you enroll in Medicare Part C, you cannot enroll in a Medigap plan. If you choose Medicare Part C (HMO or PPO) during initial enrollment and down the road decide you need a Medigap plan, you must cancel Medicare Part C and purchase traditional Medicare Parts A and B. By this time, open enrollment for Medigap has probably passed. If a health problem exists, it's uncertain whether an insurance company will sell you a Medigap plan.

Medigap will only pay for approved Medicare expenses. If your doctor, procedure, or hospital is not approved by Medicare, then neither Medicare nor Medigap will pay.

Benefits of Medigap Policies

Medigap plans help pay deductibles (the dollar amount Medicare requires patients to pay out of pocket before it begins covering remaining eligible expenses). It may also pay coinsurance costs (the expenses patients are required to pay after Medicare pays its share). Common Medicare coverage is for 80% of approved costs, leaving the patient to pay 20%. Medigap plans can help pay for those often-high expenditures.

Medigap also helps with copayment (the amount paid as the patient's share of the cost for a medical service, like a doctor or hospital outpatient visit. A copayment is usually a set amount, rather than a percentage, such as a $10 or $20 amount paid by the patient per doctor's visit or prescription.

Medigap plans offered by Medicare are required to give customers standardized coverage for each plan, meaning everyone in Medigap Plan A has the same benefit coverage, and everyone in Medigap Plan B has the same benefit coverage, and so on. Although each plan's benefits and coverage are the same, insurance companies are allowed to charge customers different premiums. Blue Cross may charge a customer one price, while Health Net may charge a different price for the same plan. Different pricing guidelines exist. Some insurance agencies base customer premiums on age.

Insurance companies offering Medigap plans are required to offer Plan A (not to be confused with **Medicare Part A**). Refer to the "Medigap Plans" chart.

Medigap plans list the percentage their plan pays toward Medicare benefits. Here are some examples:

- Medigap Plan A pays nothing for skilled-nursing facility care coinsurance, so the patient is responsible for 100% of the costs.
- Medigap Plan K pays 50% for Medicare Part B coinsurance or copay; the patient is responsible for the other 50%.

Each Medigap policy must follow federal and state laws designed to protect the consumer, and the policy must be clearly identified as "Medicare Supplement Insurance." Insurance companies can sell only a "standardized" policy identified in most states by letters. Selection and benefits vary by states.

After the open enrollment period, Medigap insurance companies are generally allowed to use medical underwriting to decide whether to accept your application and how much to charge. However, even if you have health problems, you can buy any policy during the Medigap open enrollment period when you turn sixty-five for the same price as people with good health.

Check the medicare.gov website to find insurance companies selling Medigap policies in your zip code. The following chart shows various Medigap plans and what they cover.

Medigap Plans

This chart can be found in Medicare & You 2021, the official U.S. government Medicare handbook.

BENEFITS	A	B	C*	D	F*	G**	K***	L***	M	N
Medicare Part A coinsurance and hospital costs	100%	100%	100%	100%	100%	100%	100%	100%	100%	100%
Additional 365 lifetime reserve days coinsurance and hospital costs	100%	100%	100%	100%	100%	100%	100%	100%	100%	100%
Medicare Part B coinsurance or copay	100%	100%	100%	100%	100%	100%	50%	75%	100%	****100%
Blood, first 3 pints	100%	100%	100%	100%	100%	100%	50%	75%	100%	100%
Part A hospice care coinsurance or copay	100%	100%	100%	100%	100%	100%	50%	75%	100%	100%
Skilled-nursing facility care coinsurance	No	No	100%	100%	100%	100%	50%	75%	100%	100%
Part A deductible	No	100%	100%	100%	100%	100%	50%	75%	50%	100%
Part B deductible	No	No	100%	No	100%	No	No	No	No	No
Part B excess charges	No	No	No	No	100%	100%	No	No	No	No
Foreign travel emergency (up to plan limits)	No	No	80%	80%	80%	80%	No	No	80%	80%
Out-of-pocket limit	N/A	N/A	N/A	N/A	N/A	N/A	$6,220	$3,110	N/A	N/A

NOTES

* Plans C and F are no longer offered to new enrollees of Medigap.

** Some states offer Plan G high-deductible. With this option, you must pay Medicare-covered costs (coinsurance, copayments, and deductibles) up to the deductible amount of $2,370 (for 2021) before your policy pays anything.

*** For Plans K and L, after you pay your out-of-pocket yearly limit and pay your Part B deductible ($203 for 2021), the Medigap plan pays 100% of covered services for the rest of the calendar year.

**** Plan N pays 100% of the Part B coinsurance. You must pay a copayment of up to $20 for some office visits and up to a $50 copayment for emergency room visits that don't result in an inpatient admission.

End of Medigap Plans C, F, and High-Deductible Plan F

In 2020, the US government closed Medigap Plans C, F, and High-Deductible F to new enrollees who became Medicare-eligible after January 1, 2020. People who were already plan members were grandfathered in and are able to keep their plans as long as they want.

Plan F was the most popular and comprehensive of the many Medigap insurance plans. According to research by the Kaiser Family Foundation, about 53% of people who bought Medigap supplements chose Plan C or Plan F.

The popularity of those plans made them unpopular with federal lawmakers and brought about the change. Congress decided to shut the doors on Plans C and F to reduce government Medicare spending. Although customers purchased Medigap plans from private insurance companies, critics argued Plans C and F made it too easy for people to go to a doctor without thinking twice about the cost.

Many insurance agents think Plans C and F premiums could rise as they will not be enrolling any younger, healthier people. As consumers in Plans C and F grow older and sicker, the insurance companies have the option of going to government regulators and request the right to raise rates.

Medicare Provider, Opt-Out Provider, Custodial Care

Medicare pays participating healthcare providers an approved dollar amount for patient services. This dollar amount is a much lower fee than a healthcare provider typically receives from a private insurance company or directly from a patient.

Participating providers agree to accept Medicare's approved amount for healthcare services as full payment. Nonparticipating providers accept Medicare, but they do not agree to accept the Medicare-approved amount as full payment and require patients to pay the remaining bill after Medicare pays its portion. The fee for services is a case-by-case basis.

Opt-out providers do not accept Medicare payments and have signed an agreement with Medicare to be excluded from their program. They can charge whatever they want for services but must follow certain rules. Medicare will not pay for care received from an opt-out provider except in an emergency. For a non-emergency a patient is responsible for the entire care costs. An opt-out provider must give you a private contract describing their charges and confirming that you understand you are responsible for the full costs, and Medicare will not reimburse you.

Medicare doesn't pay for nonmedical expenses for a patient's custodial care. Custodial care includes hiring personnel to assist with a person's bathing, dressing, eating, getting in and out of a bed or chair, moving around, using the bathroom, inserting eye drops, or taking prescriptions or vitamins. Custodial care can be done in a private home, nursing facility, or board and care facility.

International Medical and Travel Insurance

So many things to think about to get ready for a dream vacation! You're looking forward to a mirror image of the fabulous vacations posted by friends on Facebook. You have been doing meticulous planning because you want nothing to go wrong. No lost luggage, bad weather, canceled flights, COVID-19. But what would happen if you or a family member gets ill while on vacation? What kind of medical coverage do you have? How would you cover the cost and details of returning home? In the worst-case scenario, a family member dies. What money and resources would be needed?

Know your health coverage and options before you travel outside the US. Generally, Medicare does not provide healthcare services outside the US or onboard a ship that is more than six hours from a US port. Some Medigap policies cover travel outside the country, but coverage is limited. Check your healthcare policies for a full understanding and explanation.

Purchasing additional travel insurance is wise. Include coverage not just for lost luggage and delayed flights, but also for medical personnel, emergency room and hospital treatment, transportation, evacuation, emergency reunion, and repatriation (return of mortal remains).

A vacation is meant to be happy, but be prepared if you experience a deviation. Listed are approximate fees you might encounter in a worst-case scenario—*a death*—and the deceased must be flown home.

1. Before a deceased body is returned home, the remains must be collected and prepared. This is classified as a ship-out fee. A domestic ship-out (departure and arrival taking place in the same country) ranges from $1,000 to $3,000. This fee is to fetch the deceased from the place of death and prepare the body for shipment. Fee considerations are based on the tasks requested, such as embalming or cremation. A ship-out fee to get ready for an international (departure in one country and arrival in a different country) ranges from $3,000 to $4,000. The same tasks are performed for a domestic flight to get the deceased ready, but additional required embassy paperwork is needed.

2. Now that the remains have been prepared, there's the cost for the actual freight or transportation to bring the body home. If you are using airline cargo, the funeral shipment costs depend on the distance. Within the United States, costs vary from $600 to $3,000; international costs vary from $2,000 to $6,000.
3. The body's home. Now what? For the funeral home to receive the body from aircraft costs $1,000 to $3,000.
4. Money continues to flow. Another $500 to $10,000 is needed for funeral expenses.

Ambulance Coverage

Medicare considers an emergency to be any situation when your health is in serious danger. If a patient's health is not in immediate danger, the situation is considered a non-emergency. Medicare Part B covers ambulance services in emergencies and in limited non-emergency cases when transportation in another vehicle could endanger health.

To be covered, the patient must be transported to the nearest medical facility able to give needed care. If a patient chooses a facility farther away, Medicare pays only what it would cost to transport to the closest appropriate facility. Without insurance coverage, the cost for a short trip to the hospital by ambulance can be upward of $1,500.

Ambulance services are covered under Medicare Part B. Medicare will pay 80% of approved ambulance service charges, and the patient is responsible for 20% plus any portion of the yearly Part B deductible that has not been met.

Non-Emergency Ambulance Services

Medicare will cover non-emergency ambulance services if the ambulance supplier has received a written order from a doctor, in advance of the trip, stating that ambulance transport is medically necessary. The order must be dated no earlier than sixty days before the trip.

For unscheduled or irregular non-emergency trips, a doctor must provide a written order no later than forty-eight hours after the trip.

In limited cases, Medicare Part B covers air ambulance transportation. The service must be medically necessary and require immediate and rapid ambulance transportation that could not be provided by a ground ambulance. Air transport must meet Medicare-approved air ambulance requirements.

Louie and Lucy's stories illustrate some of the complexities of Medicare's ambulance coverage.

Lucy and Louie Opt Out

Lucy: "Louie, please don't go up on the ladder. We hired a handyman to help us once a week. He will be here tomorrow."

Louie: "Oh, Lucy, I have climbed ladders for over thirty years, including up to our second-story roof. I can change a little light bulb. You worry way too much."

Lucy: Dials 911, "My husband has fallen and can't get up." (A cliché but that's how it happened.) "Please help."

911: "Medical help is on the way."
Sirens announce the arrival of a fire truck, ambulance, and police car.

EMT: "Nothing too serious. Appears to be a fracture of his right leg. The ambulance will transport him to the hospital. Good thing he didn't climb too high."

Four days later, Louie is home, leg in a cast, and asking Lucy for lunch. Lucy opens the mail to find a $1,500 ambulance bill! After many phone calls and a surprising number of conversations with people and answering machines, Lucy discovers the ambulance was an "opt-out" Medicare provider. This means the company does not accept Medicare payments, which means Louie and Lucy are responsible for the entire $1,500 ambulance bill.

If Lucy could have had access to the good advice in this book, she would have known what it meant when the ambulance service gave her a paper stating they were an opt-out Medicare provider. Lucy would have known not to accept this company's services and would not have signed an agreement for the ambulance to transport Louie. Unrecovered money, first incident, $1,500.

Lucy—E Word (Emergency)

Poor Lucy had a second ambulance story. Another story about things that didn't go well. Louie had passed, and Lucy was living alone in a mobile home park. Late one night, Lucy twisted her ankle. She knew she needed help, so she called 911.

Lucy, a kind soul who was always thinking of others, told the operator it wasn't an emergency and not to use sirens. She didn't want the ambulance to arrive, panic everyone, and wake the sleeping.

She was relieved when the ambulance, fire truck, and police car arrived quietly. Lucy asked the ambulance driver if the ambulance service was a Medicare-approved provider. Yes, was his reply. Yeah!

Several weeks later, Lucy received a $1,500 bill from the ambulance company. How could this be? She had checked that the ambulance service was Medicare-approved, and it had taken her to a hospital only five miles away.

Numerous calls later, Lucy discovered Medicare had denied the bill because she had used the ambulance for a non-emergency. She had told the 911 operator her situation was not an emergency and not to use sirens. So much for worrying about her neighbors!

First incident	$1,500
Second incident	1,500
Total unrecovered money	$3,000

C H A P T E R   8

End-of-Life Options

Healthcare is costly, even if you have Medicare or private insurance. A 2014 report by the *Consumer Financial Protection Bureau* states 43 million Americans have overdue medical debts on their credit reports.

Healthcare can be especially expensive in the last years of a person's life, particularly if he/she is suffering from Alzheimer's disease, dementia, or any other illness that requires long-term care. This chapter can't solve the problems pertaining to healthcare expenses, but it relates information that can make you aware of some of those costs, allowing you to prepare.

Alzheimer's Disease

Alzheimer's disease is devastating, with catastrophic expenses. A person in the end stages of the disease needs help with bathing, eating, going to the bathroom (which often means changing diapers), dressing, and every activity of daily life. Help with these activities isn't considered medical costs; therefore, it isn't covered by most medical insurance plans. In some cases, people thinking ahead and planning for the years they may need to pay for assistance have purchased long-term-care insurance that helps cover these types of expenses.

According to the Alzheimer's Association, in 2019, 5.8 million Americans were living with the disease and our nation was spending $290 billion for care. The organization predicts that—without a medical breakthrough—13.8 million people will be living with Alzheimer's by the year 2050. Alzheimer's disease has continued throughout the years to be the sixth leading cause of death in the United States, and there currently is no cure or effective treatment. Sadly, the coronavirus will be a new part of death statistics for year 2020 and beyond. As demonstrated in my mother's story, Alzheimer's and dementia often lurk in plain sight. Clues are ignored because no one wants to believe that a loved

one—who may seem physically healthy—is succumbing to this dreaded disease.

Families often struggle to care for a loved one at home, hoping he/she will get better with love, attention, medication, or diet. As the disease progresses, more care is needed as the patient does less, and many families eventually find they are unable to provide extensive care. That is when families start looking for a place that can give constant care, attention, and compassion. In California, families typically have two broad options: a skilled-nursing facility or a residential care home.

Murphy's Law: Anything That Can Go Wrong, Will

It is surprising what constitutes a move to a care facility. John moved his mother, Ann, from her home in Ohio to his home in California. Ann could no longer live alone and care for herself. The family was so happy to have Ann close and a part of their home. But John's wishes to give loving care to his mother in his home were unattainable. John's house had a sunken living room. It was merely one step down. But Ann was unable to comprehend that she needed to step down when entering the living room. Despite preventive measures taken by the family, Ann fell several times. John reluctantly placed her in board and care. It is often a shock what simple complications can activate a residential placement.

Skilled-Nursing Facility

Often called nursing homes, these facilities have skilled nurses on staff around the clock in order to provide needed medical help. In addition to healthcare, these facilities offer meals and give patients help with bathing, dressing, eating, and other daily activities. Most facilities also provide for some social interaction, offering movies, bingo, card games, and more.

To find a skilled-nursing facility in your area, check the website www.medicare.gov/nursinghomecompare. On this website, you will find information on health inspections, staffing, and filed complaints.

In California (as of 2019), the basic cost for a two-person room was approximately $7,650 per month. Medicare does not pay for **long-term stays** in skilled-nursing facilities, but it often pays for **short-term rehabilitation care** in these same facilities. Medicaid may cover nursing home expenses only after a patient has exhausted the majority of his/her personal finances. Not all nursing institutions accept Medicaid. Of those that do, only a few accept Medicaid patients, since they receive less money per patient than out-of-pocket payers or those covered by long-term insurance. A Medicaid patient often has little choice about choosing a facility and may find the only available Medicaid spot is miles away from friends and family.

When receiving Medicaid help, be aware of consequences that could result. The *Medicaid Estate Recovery Program*, a provision of the 1993 *Omnibus Budget Reconciliation Act*, requires each state to recover the costs of nursing facilities and other healthcare services from the estates of Medicaid beneficiaries. This means if you were receiving Medicaid benefits for long-term care, Medicaid is permitted to file a claim against your estate after you and your spouse's death to recover some of the money the state has spent. This applies if you were over age fifty-five when receiving long-term care, or before turning fifty-five, you were permanently institutionalized. The state will not pursue funds if any minor or disabled children are entitled to your estate.

The OBRA '93 Medicaid Estate Recovery mandate provides a channel to states so they may amend their probate laws to make a Medicaid agency a priority creditor. Thus, heirs can only receive their inheritance after priority claims have been paid. An AARP September 1996 newsletter article, "Questions and Answers on Medicaid Estate Recovery for Long-Term Care Under OBRA '93," written by Faith Mullen, includes examples of applications relating to Medicaid recovering funds from an estate. Below is our own version to show what you may encounter with the application of this act.

Mr. Smith had a will and left his only property, a house valued at $75,000, to his only child, John. Yeah! John has a nice inheritance from his dad. Or does he? Let's look at John's reality. After Mr. Smith's death, the following claims and expenses were paid before the estate was closed.

John's inheritance from Dad: home value	$75,000
Bill from Medicaid for nursing home care	-24,000
Probate of estate (5% of estate value)	-3,750
Funeral expenses	-5,000
Sale of house (8% real estate commission/fees)	-6,000
John's true inheritance	**$36,250**

Residential Care Facility

This option can offer a familiar setting where the limited number of residents provides more chances for friendly interactions. The objective of group-home living is to offer compassionate care by addressing housing, social interaction, and needed assistance in clean, sanitary, healthful living accommodations. In California, residential care is limited

to six board and care residents per home.

These facilities do not offer one-on-one care, although a personal caretaker can be hired for an additional fee to address individual needs. Some residential care facilities have a dementia special-care waiver, which means the staff has been trained to manage patients with Alzheimer's or dementia.

Residential care facilities are not allowed by law to offer medical or skilled nursing, so a person needing ongoing medical treatment cannot become a resident. If a resident develops a medical condition, he/she must transfer out of the facility.

A six-unit residential care facility is typically less expensive than a skilled-nursing facility. In 2019, costs for a residential care, one-person room averaged about $4,714 per month. Skilled nursing for a two-person room was $7,650. Unfortunately, Medicaid will not pay for residential care.

Ted's Story

Are you considering a residential care facility for a loved one? Ted's story can give you a glimpse into what to expect.

Although Ted was suffering from dementia, he was able to stay in his home for a few years with a caregiver. The caregiver was awesome, but unfortunately one person can only do so much. Ted's family made the decision to place him in a six-person care facility in Simi Valley. The facility's owner owns multiple places in the area, including the home where my mom received exceptional and loving care.

Ted's family discovered that each residential care home has its own standards and costs. They also learned that any home they chose should be licensed by the California Department of Social Services, and in Ted's case, they looked for one with a dementia special-care waiver.

Before Ted could be admitted, his family had to pay a preadmission processing fee of $750. The preadmission fee covered:

- Evaluation of resident's needs
- Community maintenance
- Residential appraisal
- Staff time
- Room preparation
- Reappraisals
- Medication setup
- Employee training

- Inventory of belongings
- Dietary assessment
- Admission forms, material costs
- Legal paperwork
- Assessment of patient's required doctor's physical and evaluation

Before admission to the residence, Ted was required to have a physical and tuberculosis test. The results were documented by his doctor and a copy filed in Ted's residential placement chart. Ted's family was required to have all legal concerns addressed, including durable powers of attorney and healthcare directives.

When all requirements were completed, Ted and his personal belongings were moved to his new residence.

Ted's Approximate Monthly Costs

Monthly costs vary depending on whether a person is sharing a room and what level of care is needed. Ted's facility had level 1 through level 5. Level 1 is the least expensive and level 5 the most expensive.

At Ted's facility, a private room was $4,700 a month, and a two-person room $4,300 a month. Ted's family chose a one-person room, and Ted qualified for level 1 care. He was alert and ambulatory, able to engage in basic self-care, fully continent, emotionally stable, and had no special dietary needs.

Ted's family investigated all the levels of care offered to patients, knowing that eventually, Ted would need more hands-on care. Because many care facilities had been visited before choosing this one for Ted, his family learned to ask about the following services and determine which ones were included in the monthly fee and which ones would require extra payments.

- Monitoring and observing changes in physical, mental, emotional, and social functioning
- Notifying resident's needs to family, physician, and other appropriate persons and agencies
- Assisting in activities of daily living: dressing, eating, toileting, bathing, dispensing prescribed and over-the-counter medications, grooming, mobility
- Providing basic hygiene items such as soap, toilet paper, and latex gloves
- General laundry services such as washing and drying of personal laundry, excluding dry cleaning
- Changing bed and bath linens; how often?

- Cleaning of resident's room; how often?

Ted's family also asked questions about other specific areas and provisions.

Bathing and showering. Will residence staff help with baths and showers? How many per week are provided in the monthly cost? Can baths be given more frequently for extra charges?

Blood pressure/heart rate monitoring. In most facilities, the resident provides the equipment necessary for the staff or resident to take vital sign readings.

Food services. What food is provided, and how often? Most homes offer three nutritious meals per day plus snacks. Extra fees may be charged if a resident has a special, physician-prescribed diet.

Illnesses. Residential care facility staff do not provide full medical care, but they typically will provide bedside care and tray service for up to two days when patients suffer from minor temporary illnesses or are recovering from surgery. After two days a fee applies.

Transportation. Ted's family chose a facility that helps residents gain access or provides transportation to medical and dental appointments and social functions, such as at community centers, senior centers, or the library. Transportation options include applicable charges of $35 an hour.

Diabetics. Facilities may accept diabetic residents provided the resident is able to self-administer injectable medications, including insulin. Staff is not allowed to do injectables.

Damage fees. Fees may be charged per incident of blocking toilets or damaging light fixtures, plumbing, etc.

Third-party services. In most facilities, residents can get help from outside services for needs such as podiatry, cosmetology, or a private companion. Fees charged and collected are the responsibility of the third party.

Hospice. A residential home can give approval for a hospice agency to help care for residents who qualify for such services.

Renter's insurance. Renter's insurance was recommended to cover Ted's personal belongings.

Prescriptions, vitamins. Families should look into some kind of "facility uniform packaging," also known as "bubble packing," for delivering prescriptions to the care facility. If applicable, prescriptions can be obtained through mail order. PillPack, a full-service pharmacy, sorts medication by the prescribed dose and delivers directly to the facility's door. This type of service simplifies the process of managing medications through a combination of convenient packaging, modern technology, and personalization. If families don't use some kind of prepackaging of medications, the care facility may charge residents additional fees to handle the prescription needs. These additional costs are needed to cover the extra time used to contact pharmacies, order, and distribute medications. The facility is not responsible for paying for medications. A patient's representative's failure to provide a resident's medication may lead to prosecution of elder abuse, a criminal offense in California.

Personal items. Most care facilities expect families to supply a resident's personal toiletry articles, such as toothpaste, tissues, mouthwash, shampoo, etc. Families are also responsible for long-distance phone charges, special food products, ironing, or dry cleaning.

Palliative and Hospice Care

Palliative and hospice care are services provided for serious illnesses. This care can be provided in any setting (home or hospital). A brief description of palliative and hospice care has been included with this chapter. Explore your options and know what is available for your situation.

Palliative Care

Palliative medicine is a medical subspecialty provided by doctors. Palliative care relieves suffering and improves quality of life for people of any age and at any stage in a serious illness, whether that illness is curable, chronic, or life-threatening. The core team typically includes palliative care doctors, nurses, and social workers. This team approach is in place to offer an extra layer of full, well-rounded support (physical, emotional, and spiritual) for patients and their families.

Hospice Care

When a doctor determines a patient has six months or less to live, the patient with his/her family may choose to stop trying to cure the illness and opt to receive hospice care instead. Hospice, also called "comfort care," focuses on managing pain and keeping a patient comfortable so he/she can enjoy a good quality of life for the remainder of his/her time left. A hospice patient will not receive further medication or treatment to fight disease or prolong life.

Patients and family receive physical, emotional, and spiritual support. Just like there are many hospitals and doctors, there are also many agencies providing hospice. It is important that you investigate the agency you are considering.

Eligibility for hospice care requires two physicians certifying the patient has less than six months to live. However, in some cases, a doctor may sign an order for hospice care if the patient has a disease like Alzheimer's and their condition is deteriorating. The deciding factor can be the doctor in charge. I asked my mother's primary doctor for hospice care for her, and his answer was no. His opinion was she had a long time yet to live. She died less than four months from his statement.

Death with Dignity Laws

In California, the *End of Life Option Act* permits a terminally ill adult patient, who retains the legal capacity to make medical decisions, to ask a medical doctor to prescribe an aid-in-dying medication. When a patient meets required stipulations, a medical doctor has the authority to fulfill that request.

As of 2019, California, Colorado, the District of Columbia, Hawaii, Maine, New Jersey, Oregon, Vermont, and Washington have all passed "death with dignity" statutes. In Montana, physician-assisted dying has been legal since a 2009 state Supreme Court ruling.

Even so, it may be difficult to find a physician who will honor a patient's request. Many doctors are uncomfortable with providing such services. It may also be difficult to find a care facility that will allow a patient to choose this path in their facility.

According to California law, a request for an aid-in-dying prescription must be made solely and directly by the patient to the attending physician. The request cannot be made on behalf of the patient through a power of attorney, advance healthcare directive, conservator, healthcare agent, surrogate, or any other legally recognized healthcare decision-maker.

To make the request in California, a patient must:
- be eighteen years old or older;
- be a California resident;
- have a diagnosis from his/her primary physician of an incurable and irreversible disease that will, within reasonable medical judgment, result in death within six months;
- be capable of making medical decisions for themselves as determined by health professionals;
- voluntarily request, without others' influence, a prescription for an aid-in-dying drug;
- be able to self-administer (eat, drink, and swallow) the aid-in-dying drug.

CHAPTER 9

Funeral Planning

If you learn nothing else from this chapter, I hope you learn how important it is to discuss healthcare and funeral plans with loved ones—ideally long before you need to make decisions. Choices made ahead of a serious illness or death are easier to make as they are not clouded by stress. If you wait until you or a loved one gets very sick, you no longer have the option of clearheaded, rational discussions.

Something you should do today before a death or an emergency happens is to set up a separate bank account for emergencies. Use the funds only to specifically pay bills and expenses to keep a household running as needed or to pay funeral expenses. In case of death, the estate can't release money until issues are settled, and in some cases, a court order is needed. Make this a joint account with an executor, trustee, family member, or relative so someone has access to funds. An appropriate label would be "Account for Family Emergency or Someone's Passing." Record the information about this account with your banking notes and funeral plans. Advise your family that funds are available for emergencies.

Also consider adding this thoughtful, kind element in your funeral instructions: personal letters you have written to individual family members and friends you want to be shared after your death. Tell each person how important he/she has been in your life. We often wish, too late, we had taken more time to say "I love you" or "thank you." Write your letters **today**!

If you need more confirmation it's a good idea to do advance planning for a funeral, read Carol's story.

Carol—Happy Valley Funeral Home

Carol received a phone call from Happy Valley Funeral Home in California. The lady at the other end of the line was asking what Carol wanted to do with Ben Cooper's body. "Ben Cooper, my father?" asked Carol. Bizarre! She had no idea her father had died!

Carol called her mom, Sara, who answered the phone with a weak "hello." "Mom. Happy Valley just called and told me they are in possession of Ben Cooper's body and waiting for instructions. I'm having trouble wrapping my brain around this information."

"Oh, Carol, you have to come home. I need help! I'm sick and don't know what to do—it happened so fast. Your dad became ill with the flu, which turned into pneumonia, then a stay at the hospital, where he died. The hospital wanted to know what to do with his body. I had no clue. They suggested Happy Valley. Don't you think it sounds like a lovely place?"

Carol replied, "It would have been so motherly of you to call me with a heads-up I'm fatherless." Carol was still stunned by the ridiculousness of the situation. Her mother began sobbing.

"Mom, what about your son, Jason? He lives in the same city. Did you call him? Did you let him know Dad died?" Her mother stopped crying and replied, "Jason? The last time he was home your dad threw him out. He usually doesn't answer his phone. You know he and his girlfriend have a baby boy, Jason Jr.? His girlfriend wants him to pay child support. Jason wants to bring his girlfriend and the baby here to live."

It was clear to Carol that she was going to be stuck with all the decisions, but she didn't know when she would be able to travel. She was living in New York, and the city's transportation was paralyzed by what TV news was calling "a bomb cyclone." As a result, roads and airports were shut down.

Carol began by making funeral arrangements with Happy Valley over the phone. The clock was ticking; the price tag was rising every day her father was in Happy Valley's care. Carol decided she was glad her mom would not be choosing the casket. She would want to buy the most expensive model—the one made of indestructible steel with a luxuriant satin liner.

Although Carol remembered that her dad had once mentioned cremation, he had left no instructions about a cremation or burial. Now Happy Valley was waiting for her decisions. They asked if she wanted her dad's body to be kept in refrigeration or embalmed. Was there going to be an open casket? A viewing?

If her family had done advance planning and decided on cremation, the hospital would have called the crematory to pick up her dad. Prior to cremation, refrigeration of his body would have been provided. At the appropriate time, there would have been a cremation and the ashes returned to the family. The crematory would have taken the responsibility to file a death certificate and notify Social Security. There would be no need for Carol to scramble and pay a premium price for airline reservations. A simple memorial service could have been implemented at her arrival. No chance this seamless sequence of events was going to happen now. Carol made a mental note to prepare for more hysteria and chaos. Looking out her window at the turbulent, dismal sky, she was sure it was an omen of things to come.

Traditional Funerals—Expensive and Stressful

A traditional funeral and burial can cost $10,000 and up. If planned ahead, the cost can be less. If there is no planning, the cost can be considerably more.

After a death, family members are on a timer figuring out how to pay the expenses and make arrangements while experiencing confusion and grief. Many families think they must go through customary, impossible, expensive rituals: embalming, casket, flowers, service, burial, and social obligations. These rituals made more sense when family lived close by and were available to attend a funeral within a few days of a person's death. But today, relatives are scattered all over the world. Attending a funeral involves canceling commitments, putting employment on hold, and scheduling expensive last-minute travel.

Families put themselves through the process because they assume that their loved ones want traditional and customary funeral and burial services. But do they really? You might be surprised to find out that they would be happy with something simpler. There are many options these days. Explore some of them and discuss issues with your loved ones. You might come up with a wonderful idea that will feel just right for your family.

Celebration of Life

Some families need a funeral home and director because they need the comfort and guidance of a kind and compassionate person who will take charge. Other families see traditional funerals as expensive and stressful, with an emphasis on loss and mourning. They may also recognize the reality that the surviving spouse and children don't have a limitless budget.

More families are choosing to honor loved ones with a simple "celebration of life." What makes a celebration of life different is the level of personalization and tone. A celebration of life is not a somber affair. Instead, you find lots of laughter and storytelling.

The focus is not on the death of the person, but on the joy that the person brought to others.

An over-the-top celebration of life would be to participate in an activity or vacation the deceased would have enjoyed and to share it with friends and family.

Recompose

Eco-friendly and green are the new buzzwords for the funeral industry. In 2019, Washington became the first state to approve composting as an alternative to burying or cremating human remains. Licensed facilities are allowed to offer "natural organic reduction," which turns a body, mixed with substances such as wood chips and straw, into soil in a span of several weeks. A Seattle company, *Recompose*, is finding out that this is easier said than done. They had planned to be customer-ready in 2020 but now are looking to open sometime in 2021.

The idea seems unconventional at first, but the more you think about it, the more sense it makes. No coffin, chemicals, or fossil fuels that are needed for cremation. No need for a pricey steel casket or cemetery plot. Let's face it, no matter what casket you choose, a body is going to decompose at some point. "Recompose" appeals to religious traditions that favor simplicity and earth returning to earth.

Exploring Ideas: Helpful Information Found While Researching Our Book

Spend time exploring some of the listed resources to help you make after-death decisions.

- *Washington Post* article by Karen Heller, April 15, 2019, "The Funeral as We Know It Is Becoming a Relic—Just in Time for a Death Boom."
- Kyle Tevlin owns a business to make a celebration of life happen. Her website, *iwantafunfuneral.com*, offers workshops, planning parties, and webinars to evolve funeral plans. Participants can preplan their own funerals, conduct their own chorus, and share life event stories and life lessons on video and written logs. The object is to make a celebration of life light and fun.
- *A Good Goodbye: Funeral Planning for Those Who Don't Plan to Die* is a book by Gail Rubin that offers insights and guidance into planning a funeral. Rubin's website (https://agoodgoodbye.com) is a wealth of information: books to purchase, videos to watch (including a video of Ms. Rubin speaking at the TEDx Talks). Her TEDx Talk is light and fun. Please don't miss the opportunity to visit her website.
- *Grave Matters: A Journey through the Modern Funeral Industry to a Natural Way of Burial* by Mark Harris is a book offering insight on a natural, simplified end of life.

No matter what type of funeral and burial are chosen, the key is to discuss your wishes with loved ones. LEAVE A BLUEPRINT.

Eulogy

To write a good eulogy, start by writing an outline of a person's life. If you tackle this task early enough, it can give you and your loved ones a chance to talk and laugh together about good memories. Find out what they believe has been truly important in their lives and what they want friends and relatives to remember.

Your conversation might include these subjects:
- A brief personal history of his/her life
- Achievements
- Reflections about family, friends, and pets
- Career insights
- Important persons admired
- Favorite vacations
- Favorite book, movie, music, poem
- Hobbies and interests
- Personal stories or anecdotes
- Bucket list

Use the following worksheets. Take notes on your conversation with a loved one to create a eulogy and to help create a detailed plan for a funeral, memorial service, or celebration of life.

Eulogy Notes

Write down the important details of the conversation you have with the person the eulogy will be about.

Name _____ Date of birth _____

Information given to _____ Date _____

_____

_____

_____

_____

_____

_____

_____

_____

_____

_____

_____

_____

Eulogy

Use your notes to finalize the writing of the eulogy.

Name _____ Date of birth _____

Eulogy written by _____ Date _____

Person to give the eulogy, if known _____

_____

_____

_____

_____

_____

_____

_____

_____

_____

_____

_____

Funeral Planning
Fill out information needed for funeral

Name of individual funeral is for   Date

Person responsible for making funeral arrangements

Contact number of person responsible for funeral arrangements

Funeral home name   Contact person

Street address   City, state, zip

Phone number   Email

Website

Arrangements made to transport body to funeral home   ☐ Yes ☐ No

Name of transport service   Phone #

Burial	☐ casket ☐ cremation ☐ burial ☐ no burial ☐ entombment ☐ columbarium niche ☐ cremation garden
Service	☐ funeral home ☐ church ☐ cemetery graveside
Service preference	☐ religious ☐ nonreligious ☐ private ☐ public ☐ memorial ☐ church ☐ home ☐ Other
Celebration of life	☐ A dinner or refreshments with a gathering of relatives and friends for the purpose of sharing memories and stories of deceased.

Funeral Planning
Fill out information needed for funeral
(Continued)

Casket name

| **Material** | ☐ hardwood | ☐ metal | ☐ other | Color |

Urn name

| **Theme** | ☐ military | ☐ religious | ☐ sport | ☐ other | Color |

| **Visitation** | ☐ Yes ☐ No |

| **Casket** | ☐ Open ☐ Closed |

I'm in. I want a green burial.   Signature

I choose recomposition.
Saving the planet.
Soil instead of ashes.   Signature

Pallbearers (6)			

Military Honors	

Funeral Planning
Fill out information needed for funeral
(Continued)

Name of individual funeral is for

Clothing and jewelry selected for final appearance, if needed

Reading (favorite scriptures, poems, stories)

Music selections

Added memorabilia (flag, pictures, collage)

Flowers

Video

Funeral Planning
Fill out information needed for funeral
(Continued)

Name of individual funeral is for _____ Date _____

Person responsible for making reception arrangements _____ Phone _____

Place of reception _____

Date of reception _____ Time _____

Address _____ City, state, zip _____

Phone number _____ Email _____

Website _____

Food and refreshments _____

_____

_____

_____

_____

_____

153

Funeral Planning

Fill out information needed for funeral

(Continued)

Requested items provided by funeral home	Date	Total cost	Owed	Paid

Prepaid Funeral

Although a prepaid funeral is less expensive and easier emotionally for loved ones, there is a caveat. Know what type of funeral you want before you prepay. My husband prepaid his funeral expenses, but later changed his decision from a casket to a cremation burial. He was surprised to find he was charged $600 for the change.

Date _____

Customer prepaid funeral for _____ Phone _____

Customer address _____

Name of funeral home prepaid with _____

Address _____

Phone # _____

Funeral home representative _____ Phone _____

Transport service _____ Phone _____

Amenities	Date contracted	Total cost	Date paid in full

Total funeral costs

_____

Cemetery Planning Information

Fill out information needed for cemetery

Date

Cemetery service for

Contact person making funeral arrangements   **Phone**

Cemetery name   Contact person

Phone number   Email

Website

Street address   City, state, zip

Total cost   Prepaid ☐ Yes ☐ No

Plot #   Area name

List services paid	Date	Cost	Paid	Owed

Cemetery Planning Information
Fill out information needed for cemetery
(Continued)

Interment	☐ ground burial ☐ entombment	☐ companion plot ☐ single plot	☐ mausoleum ☐ other:	☐ single plot
Cremation	☐ companion plot ☐ mausoleum ☐ other	☐ single plot ☐ scattered ashes	☐ cremation garden ☐ columbarium niche	☐ residential urn

Type of burial marker

_____

_____

Inscription

_____

_____

_____

_____

_____

Military honors

_____

_____

_____

_____

_____

Military Funerals, Burials

Military funerals can take place in private or veteran cemeteries. Many funeral benefits are provided by the US Department of Veterans Affairs for military personnel and honorably discharged veterans. A person's military status is found on Discharge Form DD214.

Military Funeral Honors Program

Services provided for honorably discharged veterans of the US Armed Forces:

★ US flag provided at no cost, draped over the casket or to accompany the urn, given to the next of kin following the service.

★ Honor guard member to play *Taps*, a true tribute to the loved one. Veteran honor guards are volunteers giving from the heart.

★ Headstone, markers, or medallions obtained at no cost from the Department of Veterans Affairs.

★ Presidential Memorial Certificate, signed by the current president and given to the family.

California National Veterans Cemeteries

There are nine national veterans cemeteries in California. Some are full, so they are only accepting interments from veterans or eligible family members who have family members of veterans in existing gravesites. Periodically space becomes available due to disinterment. If a person's request coincides with a recently available space, the cemetery may assign it to the requesting person. Please contact the cemetery you are interested in for availability.

Since this planner is all about being prepared, it is comforting to know you can get a pre-need determination from the US Department of Veteran Affairs to see if you, your spouse, or a family member is eligible to be buried in a VA national cemetery. Once you submit an application and are approved, you or your family members can choose from an available cemetery when the time comes. Although predetermination does not guarantee burial in a specific VA national cemetery, there is no cost involved in the application process or obligation to select a VA national cemetery after approval. The VA will evaluate your burial request, considering pre-need decisions made in accordance with the laws in effect at the time of your pre-need request, including rules regarding burial benefits. Pre-approval gives you time to evaluate your situation and relieves last-minute stress decisions.

Often a military veteran and his/her family aren't aware that services and burial in a veterans cemetery are an option. Go to the US Department of Veteran Affairs, National Cemetery Administration website to get information or download an application. A funeral home can also assist in making veterans pre-need and burial arrangements.

For easy reference, California National Veterans Cemeteries are listed below. A cemetery may list its space availability as closed, but often columbarium niches have been added allowing the cemetery to accommodate cremated remains.

California National Veterans Cemeteries

Cemetery	Address	Phone	Space
Bakersfield	30338 E. Bear Mountain Blvd Arvin, CA 93203	661-867-2250 866-632-1845	Open
Fort Rosecrans	Cabrillo Memorial Dr. San Diego, CA 92106	619-553-2084	Closed
Golden Gate	1300 Sneath Ln. San Bruno, CA 94066	650-589-7737	Closed
Los Angeles	950 S. Sepulveda Blvd. Los Angeles, CA 90049	310-268-4675	Closed
Miramar	5795 Nobel Dr. San Diego, CA 92122	858-658-7360	Open
Riverside	22495 Van Buren Blvd. Riverside, CA 92518	951-653-8417	Open
Sacramento Valley	5810 Midway Rd. Dixon, CA 95620	707-693-2460	Open
San Francisco	1 Lincoln Blvd. Presidio of San Francisco San Francisco, CA 94129	650-589-7737	Closed
San Joaquin Valley	32053 W. McCabe Rd. Santa Nella, CA 95322	209-854-1040	Open

State Veterans Cemeteries

A state veterans cemetery is run by the state where the cemetery is located. Some states require a veteran's residency for burial. To learn more about California state veterans cemeteries, go to the California Veterans website: https://www.calvet.ca.gov/VetServices/Pages/Cemeteries-and-Burials.aspx. The California Department of Veterans Affairs (CalVet) provides various options for burial and memorialization at its three veterans cemeteries. On the CalVet website, there is a form and instructions to apply for predetermined eligibility for burial in a California state veterans cemetery. The application is different than the one posted on the national veterans cemetery website. The website also states this caveat, "CDVA (California Department of Veterans Affairs) will verify pre-need decisions in accordance with the laws in effect at that time." Listed below are the three California state veterans cemeteries.

California State Veterans Cemeteries

Cemetery	Address	Phone	Comments
California Central Coast Veterans Cemetery	2900 Parker Flats Rd. Seaside, CA 93955	831-393-9371	Serves all eligible veterans.
Northern California Veterans Cemetery	11800 Gas Point Rd. Igo, CA 96047	866-777-4533	This cemetery has burial space accommodations for the future 30 years and any needed expansion for 100 years. Accepting eligible veterans, spouses, eligible dependents.
Yountville Veterans Home Cemetery	260 California Ave. Yountville, CA 94599	707-944-4815	Currently accepting only interment of veterans home residents and their eligible dependents.

Proposed Southern California Cemetery

Discussions have been ongoing since 2014 regarding a proposed site for a Southern California Veterans Cemetery. Irvine and Anaheim have expressed interest.

Important Reminder

It is important to know information about military funerals and burials, but it is also important to know how to help our living veterans in their day-to-day lives. An article featured in the June 2018 *Stars and Stripes* revealed that an average of twenty military servicemen a day commit suicide, including veterans, active-duty service members, guardsmen, and reservists.

In addition, the 2019 "National Veteran Suicide Prevention Annual Report" states that a count of homeless veterans taken in January 2017 by the US Department of Housing and Urban Development found that 40,000 veterans were homeless and 15,300 were living on the streets.

Veterans and family members facing any type of mental or emotional distress should contact the **Veteran Crisis Line** at any time. **Call 800-273-8255** and **select option one** for a VA staffer. You can also text 838255 or visit VeteransCrisisLine.net for assistance.

President Abraham Lincoln promised military members that a grateful nation would "care for him who shall have borne the battle, and for his widow, and his orphan." Keeping President Abraham Lincoln's promise, among other assistance, the United States provides burial and memorial benefits to current and former members of the US Armed Forces.

Columbarium

Arlington National Cemetery Columbarium Court 2
Photo Courtesy: Elizabeth Fraser, US Army Corps of Engineers

Many burial options are offered at cemeteries, including above-ground entombment cremation sites. Niches (compartments) built into a columbarium (a wall, room, or building) are used to store urns of cremated ashes. Niches can accommodate single, double, or family remains. The name "columbarium" comes from *columba*, the Latin word for dove. Columbarium have niches that resemble those in dove houses. A columbarium can be large or small, private or public. In May 2013, Arlington National Cemetery completed construction on the 62,820-square-foot Columbarium Court 9. The new $15.6 million facility added 20,296 niches.

Tahoma National Cemetery
Kent, Washington

On October 1, 1997, the Tahoma National Cemetery opened to the public. Since the opening date, an additional two-phase construction project has been completed. Phase I, for $6 million, completed in March 2006, added 12,000 columbarium niches. Phase II, for $24 million, completed in June 2014, added 14,000 more columbarium niches and 6,000 in-ground garden cremation sites.

Edward H. Bollinger,
US Navy

Photo Courtesy: Karen Mertz

We attended Roy's brother's funeral at the awesome Tahoma National Cemetery. His ashes were placed in a columbarium niche. The ceremony was impressive and the scenery surreal.

My investigation into how military funerals work and what options are available to military families when planning a funeral led to a reacquaintance with my cousin David Opfer, an associate member of the President Ronald Reagan Detachment #597, Marine Corps League, Color Guard/Honor Guard.

The detachment members work voluntarily out of Simi Valley, California, providing military funeral honors to eligible veterans. We are in awe of the commitment provided by David and this brigade of soldiers. All services rendered are without compensation for travel, gas, or purchasing of required uniforms.

Military.com presents a description of the responsibilities that this detachment provides:

> An honor guard detail for the burial of an eligible veteran consists of not fewer than two members of the Armed Forces. One member of the detail represents the parent service of the deceased veteran.
>
> The honor detail will, at a minimum, perform a ceremony that includes the folding and presenting of the American flag to the next of kin and the playing of taps. When available, taps will be played by a bugler; however, there are so few buglers available that the military services may choose to provide an electronic recording of taps. The veteran's parent service representative will present the flag.

President Ronald Reagan Detachment 597, Marine Corps League, not only provides services for funerals, but they also represent the military on many holiday and civic occasions: Ronald Reagan Presidential Library functions, Veterans Day, Memorial Day, Presidents' Day, Toys for Tots, and city and state events. This group recently participated in Gunnery Sgt. Diego Pongo's memorial parade in Simi Valley. Gunnery Sgt. Diego was killed in Iraq while on duty.

David is proud of the opportunities he has had to meet many individuals who have honored and continue to honor our nation with their service.

Gary Sinise book signing of Grateful American *for David Opfer at Reagan Presidential Library*

Brigadier General Kevin J. Killea and David Opfer at Ronald Reagan Presidential Library

Military Funeral Planning

Consult the US Department of Veterans Affairs, state veterans cemeteries,
or a funeral home for details regarding military memorial services and burials.
This is a wonderful service provided to veterans, but it requires advance planning.
Use the following worksheet to get all your information in one place.

First, middle, last name of veteran

Location of military discharge papers DD214

Maiden name or other
name(s) used on active duty   Date of birth

Rank   Branch of service

Service serial number   Social Security #

Date entered active service   Place

Date discharged   Place

Conflicts/wars served

Medals/honors/citations

State of residency

Name of cemetery of interest

☐ National veterans cemetery   ☐ State veterans cemetery   ☐ Public cemetery with military honors
☐ Ground Burial   ☐ Cremation   ☐ Columbarium niche   ☐ Cremation garden

Deceased entitled to a free burial flag?   ☐ Yes   ☐ No

To apply for a veteran's burial flag, complete VA Form 27-2008, found on
http://www.benefits.va.gov website. A funeral director can help you with this process.

After-Death Checklist
Checklist of items needing attention immediately after a death.

✓	**Death at Home Checklist**
	Call 911.
	If the person was on hospice care, notify hospice and ask for instructions.
	Check wishes regarding organ donation and follow procedures.

✓	**Death in Hospital/Nursing Home/Board and Care Checklist**
	Check wishes regarding organ donation and follow procedures.
	Optimal scenario. Family instructions and chosen mortuary are on file at the patient's current hospital, nursing home, or board and care. The healthcare facility will follow instructions and contact the appropriate establishment to take possession of the body.

✓	**Notifications Checklist**
	Notify family and community members. Filling out the included worksheets in advance will help make this task much easier.
	Review funeral and burial plans with the spouse and children.
	Make arrangements for cremation, if applicable.
	Decide on burial clothes, if applicable.

✓	**Plan Services Checklist**
	Choose a picture and/or a life video of the deceased to display for services.
	Choose music.
	Choose six pallbearers, if applicable.

Set Up Meeting with Chosen Mortuary Checklist

✓	
	Now is your chance to shine. Bring your notebook with prepaid funeral and burial plans.
	Implement pre-burial steps.
	Decide on services, burial date, and time.
	Pay the balance of any items not locked in.
	Request appropriate number of certified copies of death certificates for your situation. Twelve to fifteen certified copies are often needed.
	Select flowers, register book, and memorial cards.
	Confirm casket/urn/vault/niche.
	If applicable, select clergy: priest, rabbi, minister, or imam.
	Give the person in charge a copy of the eulogy, video, and music to play.
	Set a date and time for the viewing, if applicable.
	Decide if and where you are having a meal or refreshments after the service.
	Prepare a menu of foods and drinks.
	Locate and have available accessories: family photos, videos, and music.
	Reserve home, reception room, or restaurant.
	Confirm the burial date and time the mortuary arranged with the cemetery.
	Prepay open/close costs and other required expenses.
	Decide if chairs/canopy are needed.
	Confirm the burial plot location and number. Notify family members, friends, and coworkers of the date, time, and place of services. Refer to your notification list.

Order Headstone or Plaque Checklist
(Granite is recommended for longevity)

✓	
	Choose the color.
	Choose the design/inscription.
	Confirm the installation date.
	Pay for the plaque/headstone and inscription.

Notification of Passing
Family Members, Friends, Coworkers

Name of deceased _____

Contacted ☐ Yes ☐ No   Name _____

Relationship _____ Cell phone _____

Email _____ Home phone _____

Street address _____ City, state, zip _____

Contacted ☐ Yes ☐ No   Name _____

Relationship _____ Cell phone _____

Email _____ Home phone _____

Street address _____ City, state, zip _____

Contacted ☐ Yes ☐ No   Name _____

Relationship _____ Cell phone _____

Email _____ Home phone _____

Street address _____ City, state, zip _____

Contacted ☐ Yes ☐ No   Name _____

Relationship _____ Cell phone _____

Email _____ Home phone _____

Street address _____ City, state, zip _____

Contacted ☐ Yes ☐ No   Name _____

Relationship _____ Cell phone _____

Email _____ Home phone _____

Street address _____ City, state, zip _____

Notification of Passing
Family Members, Friends, Coworkers
(Continued)

Name of deceased _____

Contacted ☐ Yes ☐ No   Name _____

Relationship _____   Cell phone _____

Email _____   Home phone _____

Street address _____   City, state, zip _____

Contacted ☐ Yes ☐ No   Name _____

Relationship _____   Cell phone _____

Email _____   Home phone _____

Street address _____   City, state, zip _____

Contacted ☐ Yes ☐ No   Name _____

Relationship _____   Cell phone _____

Email _____   Home phone _____

Street address _____   City, state, zip _____

Contacted ☐ Yes ☐ No   Name _____

Relationship _____   Cell phone _____

Email _____   Home phone _____

Street address _____   City, state, zip _____

Contacted ☐ Yes ☐ No   Name _____

Relationship _____   Cell phone _____

Email _____   Home phone _____

Street address _____   City, state, zip _____

Notification of Passing
Family Members, Friends, Coworkers
(Continued)

Name of deceased _____

Contacted ☐ Yes ☐ No   Name _____

Relationship _____   Cell phone _____

Email _____   Home phone _____

Street address _____   City, state, zip _____

Contacted ☐ Yes ☐ No   Name _____

Relationship _____   Cell phone _____

Email _____   Home phone _____

Street address _____   City, state, zip _____

Contacted ☐ Yes ☐ No   Name _____

Relationship _____   Cell phone _____

Email _____   Home phone _____

Street address _____   City, state, zip _____

Contacted ☐ Yes ☐ No   Name _____

Relationship _____   Cell phone _____

Email _____   Home phone _____

Street address _____   City, state, zip _____

Contacted ☐ Yes ☐ No   Name _____

Relationship _____   Cell phone _____

Email _____   Home phone _____

Street address _____   City, state, zip _____

Notification of Passing
Attorney, Doctors, Dentists, Professional Contacts

Name of deceased

Contacted	☐ Yes ☐ No	Name
Profession		Cell phone
Email		Home phone

Contacted	☐ Yes ☐ No	Name
Profession		Cell phone
Email		Home phone

Contacted	☐ Yes ☐ No	Name
Profession		Cell phone
Email		Home phone

Contacted	☐ Yes ☐ No	Name
Profession		Cell phone
Email		Home phone

Contacted	☐ Yes ☐ No	Name
Profession		Cell phone
Email		Home phone

Contacted	☐ Yes ☐ No	Name
Profession		Cell phone
Email		Home phone

Notification of Passing
Attorney, Doctors, Dentists, Professional Contacts
(Continued)

Name of deceased _____

Contacted ☐ Yes ☐ No   Name _____

Profession _____ Cell phone _____

Email _____ Home phone _____

Contacted ☐ Yes ☐ No   Name _____

Profession _____ Cell phone _____

Email _____ Home phone _____

Contacted ☐ Yes ☐ No   Name _____

Profession _____ Cell phone _____

Email _____ Home phone _____

Contacted ☐ Yes ☐ No   Name _____

Profession _____ Cell phone _____

Email _____ Home phone _____

Contacted ☐ Yes ☐ No   Name _____

Profession _____ Cell phone _____

Email _____ Home phone _____

Contacted ☐ Yes ☐ No   Name _____

Profession _____ Cell phone _____

Email _____ Home phone _____

Visitation, Funeral, Burial Service Details and/or Memorial

It is hard to remember all the details at a stressful time with a lot of activity going on. This worksheet may help you keep everyone on track, yourself included.

Name of deceased _____ Date _____

Visitation date and time _____

    Place _____

    Address _____

    Person in charge _____

    Contact phone # _____

Funeral date and time _____

    Place _____

    Address _____

    Person in charge _____

    Contact phone # _____

Burial services date and time _____

    Place _____

    Address _____

    Person in charge _____

    Contact phone # _____

Memorial date and time _____

    Place _____

    Address _____

    Person in charge _____

    Contact phone # _____

Newspaper Death, Obituary Notices

Newspaper obituaries and death notices are another time-honored tradition that may give you sticker shock.

Carrie was beyond surprised. Her mom had died suddenly, and Carrie had to make many decisions very quickly, so she didn't think twice when she ordered a newspaper obituary. But she definitely had second thoughts when she received a bill for $300 from the local newspaper!

Armed with more information and time, Carrie would have discovered she really didn't need a printed obit for her mom because the funeral home provides an online obit FREE with their funeral package. Online obituaries may be included in funeral home packets and are common on Facebook, and in emails, and text messages.

If you still want a notice to appear about your loved one's death in your local paper, check their rates and know that most papers carry two kinds of notices.

Death Notice

A death notice is a simple statement of death: announcing the person has died, information on the funeral service, where donations can be made in the name of the person, and minor biographical information. When submitted, a death notice must be accompanied by proof of death. These notices may be free or may be much cheaper than a full obituary.

Obituary

Historically an obituary (obit) was written by a newspaper staff member, but these days in most cases, family members are responsible for supplying them to newspapers. An obituary contains more information than a death notice and typically includes details about the deceased's life. It may include a picture.

Average obituary costs are between $200 and $500. Some newspapers charge by the line and may charge more to add a photograph. All obituary requests must be accompanied by proof of death. Funeral home directors typically arrange for death notices and obituaries to be printed in local newspapers. A death notice or obituary is not required by law.

If applicable, use the following worksheet to help put together a death notice or obituary to submit to a local paper.

Death Notice, Obituary

Date

Name of deceased

Newspaper(s) where death notice and/or obituary should appear, include ad cost

Online obituary

Attached photo

Information to be included in death notice or obituary

CHAPTER 10

Surviving Spouse
Action Plan

Dealing with the death of a spouse can be one of the most difficult tasks of your life. At a time when grief and confusion cloud your every waking moment, you are expected to take steps and make decisions that can affect your legal and financial future for years to come.

You will find stories in this chapter of real people who have faced these challenges. Some of them have made costly mistakes, and we share their stories so you can learn from those mistakes and avoid them.

Completed worksheets in this chapter will guide you through these dark days. Use the worksheets to keep track of important information, remind yourself of the progress you have made, and see what tasks still need to be completed.

It is important, for this chapter and the next, to keep a designated notebook. Use this notebook to log contacts and contact information as you progress through responsibilities. *Keep track of all communication.* Enter *date, issue* (the problem and what answers you need), *person(s) you talked to*, and *what was said.* You will be surprised how many telephone calls and emails may be needed to resolve one issue and how many people you will talk to and different answers you will receive.

If you have no one to help you, feel overwhelmed, or need help going through all the paperwork to close your deceased spouse's estate, consider hiring a lawyer or personal financial advisor. *But be vigilant. Don't trust your information and finances to just anyone.*

Members of the National Association of Personal Financial Advisors must sign a yearly *fiduciary oath* and subscribe to a *code of ethics.* You can find out more information about their organization and how to find a personal financial advisor in your area at www.napfa.org, or call 888-333-6659.

Deceased Personal Information

Fill in all applicable information.

Full legal name

Maiden name

Nickname

Phone #

Street address

City, state, zip

Date of birth

Date of death

Death location

Social Security #

Birthplace (city, state)

Marriage date, if applicable

Divorce date, if applicable

Father of deceased name

Father's date of birth

Father's birthplace

Father's date of death, if applicable

Father's location of death, if applicable

Mother of deceased name

Deceased Personal Information

Fill in all applicable information.
(Continued)

Mother's maiden name

Mother's date of birth

Mother's birthplace

Mother's date of death, if applicable

Mother's location of death, if applicable

Death Certificates

All deaths are required to be recorded with your local or state vital records office. For a death in California, you can request official death certificates from the California Department of Public Health–Vital Records, or when working with a funeral home or mortuary, they can order them for you. The cost for each certified death certificate purchased from the California Department of Public Health–Vital Records is $21 (in 2020). Costs for a certified copy of a death certificate varies for each state. Death certificates are needed in more places than you expect. To make sure you're covered, you may want to purchase twelve to fifteen copies.

There are many private vendors online providing services to obtain death certificates for the public. Be aware purchases from these vendors are much more expensive per certificate.

When you get the certified copies, make at least ten extra copies for institutions that do not require a certified copy of the death certificate. Insurance companies and other organizations may also ask for birth, death, and marriage certificates. Be prepared to supply needed requests.

Social Security and Medicare

Family members are legally responsible to notify the Social Security Administration (SSA) when a Social Security or Medicare member dies. The SSA will pass the information on to Medicare. Call 800-772-1213 to inform the SSA of the death. Traditionally, a mortuary or funeral home also provides this information to the SSA, but you should check to see if this task has been completed. The deceased's Social Security payments will be terminated, and the surviving spouse's Social Security checks may be affected as well.

When you call, be sure to ask the SSA representative to reevaluate the surviving spouse's monthly benefit. If the deceased spouse received a higher monthly dollar amount, the surviving spouse may now be entitled to receive that amount.

Death Benefit

If you are the surviving spouse, when you call the SSA, ask the representative if you qualify for the $255 (in 2020) lump-sum-burial-benefit. If there is no surviving spouse, a surviving child may be eligible to receive the benefit if he/she meets the qualifying rules. The estate is not entitled to receive a death benefit from Social Security when the second spouse dies.

Social Security monthly checks are normally paid by direct deposit to a financial institution or by a Direct Express Card. No check is payable for the month of death, even if the person dies on the last day of the month. Social Security will reclaim any money the recipient was not entitled to.

Social Security, Medicare Notification

Deceased name
_____

Social Security #
_____

Surviving spouse name
_____

Social Security #
_____

Social Security representative name
_____

Social Security representative ID/title
_____

Date of conversation
_____

Notes
_____

_____

Susan and Bill—Consequences of Living in the Moment

Fifteen years of marriage ended with the D words—Dreaded Divorce. In the divorce agreement, Bill was awarded the house he and Susan had purchased together. Susan moved out. Bill removed Susan's name from the title.

A couple of years later, realizing their marriage had not been a complete disaster, Susan moved back into the home with Bill. They lived happily together for the next ten years. Not seeing the need, they never remarried.

Susan became Suzy Homemaker: painting, cooking, cleaning, gardening. She devoted all her time and energy to Bill and their home. This idealistic picture ended when Bill was diagnosed with cancer. Susan spent the next year nursing him with loving care until his death.

Consequence #1

Since Susan and Bill were not married at the time of his death, Susan was not entitled to his $255 Social Security death benefit, even though she accepted responsibility for all burial expenses.

Consequence #2

Bill did not have a will or trust; he had never thought about it. Susan had never thought about it either until she received a letter from a lawyer stating that Paul, Bill's son by a previous marriage, had petitioned the court for a letter of authority to administer Bill's estate. Paul demanded Susan immediately move out of Bill's house, claiming ownership by intestate succession—a child's right to inherit the estate of the deceased. He had that right even though Paul hadn't seen his father in more than ten years and did not attend his funeral.

Bill and Susan had overlooked many options that would have led to a better outcome for Susan. They could have:

- remarried, giving Susan spousal rights;
- created a will or trust;
- put Susan's name back on the house title; or
- given Susan a legal claim to the estate by filing a declaration of domestic partnership with the California Secretary of State. A legal declaration of domestic partnership offers partners in a relationship similar rights as married partners, including inheritance and visitation privileges in jails and hospitals.

Declaration of Domestic Partnership

Domestic partnerships can be entered into by male + male, female + female, and male + female couples. All participants must be at least 18 years of age (with some exceptions). Until January 1, 2020, when California Senate Bill 30 took effect, in a female + male relationship, one of the partners would have had to be at least 62 years of age.

Living in California, filing a domestic partnership would have been an option for Bill and Susan, both meeting the 2019 age criterion. The downside of this type of agreement is that federal law does not recognize these relationships. Only California, Oregon, Maine, Hawaii, the District of Columbia, and Nevada have passed state laws legalizing domestic partnership contracts in their states (as of 2020).

A domestic partner is not entitled to a Social Security lump-sum death benefit.

Other Important Notifications

Medi-Cal

Once the Social Security Administration is notified of a death, if applicable, the information becomes part of Medicaid and Medicare records. No other action needs to be taken to alert Medicaid of the death. Many times this task is completed by a funeral home director.

County Assessor Office

Whenever there is a change in ownership of real property, the county assessor office must be notified. When a person dies and owns real property, the county assessor office must be notified within 150 days of the date of death. A **Change in Ownership Statement (Death of Real Property Owner)** must be filed with their office. If the estate is probated, notification can be done at the same time the estate inventory and appraisal are filed. This is very important. A severe penalty could be incurred for non-compliance. Call the county assessor office in your area to determine the needed paperwork.

County Assessor Office

Name of county assessor office

Assessor office telephone number

Forms needed

Date assessor office notified

Financial Accounts

Remove deceased's name from each checking, savings, and certificate of deposit (CD) account. If you have bills or other payments being withdrawn automatically from an account, make sure the auto-pay settings are adjusted correctly.

Set up new primary beneficiaries on each account. If you have a trust, you may not want to include your checking and savings accounts in the trust, but you may want to include CDs. For accounts you want to include, make the trust the second beneficiary and retitle accounts into the name of the trust to avoid probate.

Financial Accounts Worksheet

Use the following worksheet to help keep track of closed financial accounts of the deceased and if applicable established new ones.

Deceased name   Institution

Account number   Account value

User name   Password

Date deceased removed from account

Beneficiary/beneficiaries

New account holder name   Institution

New account number   New account value

User name   Password

New beneficiary/beneficiaries

Deceased name   Institution

Account number   Account value

User name   Password

Date deceased removed from account

Beneficiary/beneficiaries

New account holder name   Institution

New account number   New account value

User name   Password

New beneficiary/beneficiaries

Financial Accounts Worksheet
(Continued)

Deceased name

Institution

Account number

Account value

User name

Password

Date deceased removed from account

Beneficiary/beneficiaries

New account holder name

Institution

New account number

New account value

User name

Password

New beneficiary/beneficiaries

Deceased name

Institution

Account number

Account value

User name

Password

Date deceased removed from account

Beneficiary/beneficiaries

New account holder name

Institution

New account number

New account value

User name

Password

New beneficiary/beneficiaries

Medical, Drug, Dental, Vision Insurance Plans

Notify each medical plan of your spouse's death. If you are insured under your deceased spouse's plan, you may have only thirty days to convert to a COBRA plan. Ask your insurance company representatives how much longer you are covered under your deceased spouse's insurance. If the deceased spouse was on your insurance plan, remove him/her as it may lower your premiums.

Use the following worksheet to help keep track of your insurance accounts, and which accounts need to be addressed.

Insurance Accounts Worksheet

Name of insurance plan   Phone number

Person insured

ID number   Date talked to agent

Agent's name

Name of insurance plan   Phone number

Person insured

ID number   Date talked to agent

Agent's name

Name of insurance plan   Phone number

Person insured

ID number   Date talked to agent

Agent's name

Insurance Accounts Worksheet
(Continued)

Name of insurance plan _____ Phone number _____

Person insured _____

ID number _____ Date talked to agent _____

Agent's name _____

Name of insurance plan _____ Phone number _____

Person insured _____

ID number _____ Date talked to agent _____

Agent's name _____

Name of insurance plan _____ Phone number _____

Person insured _____

ID number _____ Date talked to agent _____

Agent's name _____

Name of insurance plan _____ Phone number _____

Person insured _____

ID number _____ Date talked to agent _____

Agent's name _____

Hospital, Healthcare Facilities, Related Healthcare

Be sure to contact all hospitals, skilled-nursing facilities, rehab centers, ambulance companies, and any other healthcare facilities or organizations where your spouse may have been treated. Find out if there is a balance owed on any account, or if you are entitled to a refund. Then file any necessary insurance claims for those services. Use the following worksheet to help you.

Healthcare Facilities

Name of
medical account _____   Account ID number _____

Contact number _____   Web address _____

PIN/password _____   Account
balance paid _____

Payment or
refund amount _____

Name of
medical account _____   Account ID number _____

Contact number _____   Web address _____

PIN/password _____   Account
balance paid _____

Payment or
refund amount _____

Name of
medical account _____   Account ID number _____

Contact number _____   Web address _____

PIN/password _____   Account
balance paid _____

Payment or
refund amount _____

Healthcare Facilities
(Continued)

Name of
medical account _____ Account ID number _____

Contact number _____ Web address _____

PIN/password _____ Account
balance paid _____

Payment or
refund amount _____

Name of
medical account _____ Account ID number _____

Contact number _____ Web address _____

PIN/password _____ Account
balance paid _____

Payment or
refund amount _____

Name of
medical account _____ Account ID number _____

Contact number _____ Web address _____

PIN/password _____ Account
balance paid _____

Payment or
refund amount _____

Name of
medical account _____ Account ID number _____

Contact number _____ Web address _____

PIN/password _____ Account
balance paid _____

Payment or
refund amount _____

Other Accounts, Memberships, House Title

Remove deceased's name from the house title, home loans, and house insurance.

Be sure to cancel unwanted subscriptions and memberships to newspapers, magazines, and health clubs of the deceased spouse. Ask for a partial refund on unused portions of subscriptions and memberships.

Also notify utilities, trash collection, post office, and homeowner's association of the deceased spouse's death, and remove his/her name from the accounts. Check to see if you should adjust auto-pay arrangements for any account.

Although it seems obvious, you should continue to make mortgage, insurance, and loan-related payments as necessary. Check your financial situation, as your income and expenses have changed. Prepare a list of all your monthly income and expenses. Include in your list of expenses all insurance costs, taxes, etc.

Life Insurance and Annuity Policies

Call each of the deceased's insurance and annuity policy providers to request beneficiary information, the policy value for each beneficiary, and the process for receiving funds. Check with your late spouse's employer regarding any life insurance policy he/she may have had through employment.

If the deceased is a listed beneficiary of your work life insurance policy or other policies, remove his/her name and set up a new beneficiary/beneficiaries. You will probably want to make your children the primary beneficiaries. Be sure to state the percentage of funds you want to go to each child. If you have a trust, make the trust the second beneficiary. Life insurance payouts are generally not taxable.

If you cash out an annuity, the annuity earnings will be taxed as ordinary income. Have the insurance company withhold a certain percentage of money for payment of federal and state taxes.

If you are not sure whether you are entitled to any other private insurance policies your spouse held, browse through checkbook registers, canceled checks, and credit card statements looking for payments made to insurance companies. Also check with your banks and credit unions for any $1,000 policies that are often opened automatically for customers.

Use the following charts and worksheets to help with this task.

Life Insurance and Annuity Policies

Insurance company	Insurance policy number

Agent contact phone

Beneficiaries

Issue maturity date	Date of death value	Date paid out

Insurance company	Insurance policy number

Agent contact phone

Beneficiaries

Issue maturity date	Date of death value	Date paid out

Insurance company	Insurance policy number

Agent contact phone

Beneficiaries

Issue maturity date	Date of death value	Date paid out

Insurance company	Insurance policy number

Agent contact phone

Beneficiaries

Issue maturity date	Date of death value	Date paid out

Life Insurance and Annuity Policies

(Continued)

Insurance company | Insurance policy number

Agent contact phone

Beneficiaries

Issue maturity date | Date of death value | Date paid out

Insurance company | Insurance policy number

Agent contact phone

Beneficiaries

Issue maturity date | Date of death value | Date paid out

Insurance company | Insurance policy number

Agent contact phone

Beneficiaries

Issue maturity date | Date of death value | Date paid out

Insurance company | Insurance policy number

Agent contact phone

Beneficiaries

Issue maturity date | Date of death value | Date paid out

Company Pensions and Wages

If your spouse was working or retired and receiving a pension, be sure to notify his/her employer of his/her death. If he/she was receiving a pension, ask if you will continue receiving pension payments and for how long. Will you receive full, reduced, or no pension payments?

If the deceased was still employed, ask if any unpaid wages are due to his/her spouse.

If you have trouble finding the correct employee ID for your late spouse, look on a pay or pension check.

If you have a pension, notify your company of your spouse's death. Will taking your deceased spouse off your pension plan increase the amount of money you are or will be receiving?

Use the following worksheet to help make sure you have the pertinent information regarding your late spouse's pay or pension.

Deceased Spouse Employment and Pension History

Name of company	Employee ID	Date contacted
Contact number	Monthly value	
Web address	Password	
Name of company	Employee ID	Date contacted
Contact number	Monthly value	
Web address	Password	
Name of company	Employee ID	Date contacted
Contact number	Monthly value	
Web address	Password	

Deceased Spouse Employment
and Pension History
(Continued)

Name of company	Employee ID	Date contacted
Contact number	Monthly value	
Web address	Password	
Name of company	Employee ID	Date contacted
Contact number	Monthly value	
Web address	Password	
Name of company	Employee ID	Date contacted
Contact number	Monthly value	
Web address	Password	
Name of company	Employee ID	Date contacted
Contact number	Monthly value	
Web address	Password	
Name of company	Employee ID	Date contacted
Contact number	Monthly value	
Web address	Password	

Bob and Ruth's 20-Year Whammy!

People do not realize how important it is to know their pension entitlement. Who in your family is entitled to receive a pension? Is the pension passed on to another person when the original pension holder dies? Checking on a deceased spouse's pension coverage is one of the most important tasks a survivor must execute.

When Ruth's husband, Bob, died, he was receiving a monthly pension check, which Ruth assumed ended with his death. In addition, Ruth and Bob each received monthly Social Security income. After Bob's death, Ruth elected to receive Bob's monthly Social Security payment, since his money allotment was higher than hers. This action canceled her Social Security entitlement. A surviving spouse can only receive one Social Security benefit, not two.

Assuming Bob's pension ended with his death, Ruth's only income was now Bob's monthly Social Security allotment. Ruth struggled financially. Savings were small and quickly depleted. She was forced to sell her home, not having enough money for taxes and upkeep.

Ruth lived for ten years after Bob's death. When she died, their children made a distressing discovery regarding Bob's pension. Bob had chosen to take a smaller dollar amount for each monthly check so that Ruth would continue receiving his pension after his death. The children wondered if Ruth even might have been entitled to receive health benefits. They contacted the pension holder, asking if the money Ruth had never been paid could be recovered and passed on to her heirs. Unfortunately, only Bob's widow had been entitled to receive the funds. Entitlement ended with her death.

A two-fisted, twenty-year punch on Bob and Ruth's finances! 1) For ten years, Bob and Ruth had lived on a reduced pension dollar amount. 2) For ten more years, Ruth did not receive Bob's entitled pension.

Claiming Pension Benefits

Ruth's unclaimed pension is more common than you might imagine. The Pension Benefit Guaranty Corporation website gives us the following information. In the 2018, 80,000 people in the United States had not claimed pension benefits. Those unclaimed benefit were worth over $300 million. At $40.6 million, California topped the list of states with the highest amount of unclaimed pensions.

Bob and Ruth's experience could happen to you. Companies with pension plans don't go out of their way to defraud employees, but mistakes are easily made. Clerical help in the retirement division are just paper-pushers. They only see the obvious; if paper-

work wasn't filed for Ruth claiming Bob's pension, there would be no red flag telling the clerk to send a pension check to Ruth. And consider that a pension plan may not purposely want to cheat you, but there is no incentive for them to pay clerical help to catch mistakes when uncollected pension money stays on the books.

There are many reasons people fail to claim their earned benefits. Sometimes people forget about pension plans at previous employers, particularly when retirees move to a new location. It can also happen when a company or office:

- closes or consolidates its operations elsewhere;
- is bought by another company and given a new name;
- merges with another company;
- divides into separate parts, none of which retain the old company name;
- goes bankrupt or simply closes its doors and disappears; or any combination of the above.

The Pension Benefit Guaranty Corporation (PBGC) is available to help protect pension benefits, even if a company goes out of business or lacks the funds to pay its commitments. The PBGC website can be used to search for an organization by company name or the state where the company had been headquartered. Good news. From 1995 to 2007, the PBGC regained $137 million worth of lost pensions for 22,000 people. For 2,621 Californians, $8.33 million was recovered. Listed below are two agencies that are helpful if you need pension information or need to search for unclaimed property.

Pensions

Pension Benefit Guaranty Corporation: www.pbgc.gov

Monday–Friday, except federal holidays, 8 a.m.–7 p.m. EST

800-400-7242

Unclaimed Property

California State Controller: sco.ca.gov

Credit and Debit Cards

A financial institution will immediately cancel credit and debit cards when notified the holder has died. You need to notify all credit/debit card companies of your spouse's death, even if you are a joint holder on the account, as the card is no longer for your use.

Check the balance owed and determine what obligations need to be met. Are automatic payments set up from bank accounts that you are also closing or changing? If so, be sure to make other auto-pay arrangements. Confirm cancellations are completed.

Name of company	Account number
Amount owed	Amount paid
Date	Contact number
Website	Online account password
Name of company	Account number
Amount owed	Amount paid
Date	Contact number
Website	Online account password
Name of company	Account number
Amount owed	Amount paid
Date	Contact number
Website	Online account password

Credit and Debit Cards
(Continued)

Name of company	Account number
Amount owed	Amount paid
Date	Contact number
Website	Online account password
Name of company	Account number
Amount owed	Amount paid
Date	Contact number
Website	Online account password
Name of company	Account number
Amount owed	Amount paid
Date	Contact number
Website	Online account password
Name of company	Account number
Amount owed	Amount paid
Date	Contact number
Website	Online account password

Sally Learns Cash Is King

Sally's husband Tom was hit by a car and killed while riding his bike to work. Tom's head injuries were extensive, even though he had been wearing his newly purchased $500 helmet. Sally had protested. "Isn't there a less expensive one? The children need shoes." Tom's reply, "You want me safe, don't you, honey?"

A few weeks later, Sally was looking forward to sharing a quiet weekend with the kids. All of them were still struggling with their shock and loss. While collecting the kids from day care, Sally was informed her check had bounced for this month's tuition. She promised to look into it, and the day care employee kindly didn't press the discussion.

Sally just wanted to get home and end this day, but like Mother Hubbard, her cupboards were bare. She stopped at the grocery store with four-year-old Billy and two-year-old Kathy. Every food advertised in kids' television commercials was added to her overflowing cart. She searched for her favorite cheerful clerk's checkout register. She was a godsend, always engaging the kids and pretending not to notice mouths full of candy and sticky hands.

Mission nearly accomplished. Groceries bagged, children fighting over a cereal box. Then the clerk's look of pity, an omen of what was to come, as she blurted out, "Sorry, your credit card has been denied." Tears gushed from Sally's eyes. Customers looked at her. She knew she looked as unglued as she felt. Billy and Kathy intuitively were drawn to their mother's distress, and immediately mother, son, and daughter became a sobbing chorus.

Whammy Times Two

Sally had been foiled by a little-understood policy that allows only one owner of a credit card account. Additional "authorized users" may be added to an account and can get a separate card in the user's name. But if the owner of the account dies, the cards are canceled and additional users lose their authorization.

The second whammy may come when the surviving spouse applies for a new credit card. Because finances have changed for the surviving spouse, the new account may have a lower credit limit and a higher interest rate. To avoid this problem, make sure each spouse is the primary holder of at least one credit card.

And remember that *cash is king.* It is imperative to have a separate savings account available for emergency use.

Loans

Notify all creditors of the death of a loan holder. If you are both named on a loan, remove the deceased's name. If the loan is in the deceased's name only, notify the creditor of the death and check to see what your liability is to continue payments.

Also report the death in writing to the Equifax, Experian, and TransUnion credit bureaus. Financial experts at Credit.com recommend you send each of the credit bureaus a letter that includes your name, contact information, and relationship to the deceased. Include the deceased's Social Security number, last address, date of birth, and date of death, and a copy of the death certificate. Request the agency deny any new credit in the deceased's name.

Loans

Name of company

Account number

Amount owed

Amount paid

Date

Contact number

Website

Online account password

Name of company

Account number

Amount owed

Amount paid

Date

Contact number

Website

Online account password

Name of company

Account number

Amount owed

Amount paid

Date

Contact number

Website

Online account password

Name of company

Account number

Amount owed

Amount paid

Date

Contact number

Website

Online account password

Loans

(Continued)

Name of company _____   Account number _____

Amount owed _____   Amount paid _____

Date _____   Contact number _____

Website _____   Online account password _____

Name of company _____   Account number _____

Amount owed _____   Amount paid _____

Date _____   Contact number _____

Website _____   Online account password _____

Name of company _____   Account number _____

Amount owed _____   Amount paid _____

Date _____   Contact number _____

Website _____   Online account password _____

Name of company _____   Account number _____

Amount owed _____   Amount paid _____

Date _____   Contact number _____

Website _____   Online account password _____

Safe Deposit Box, Home Safe

When a safe deposit box is held jointly between spouses, the surviving spouse can access it in the same manner as if the decedent had not died. This is a general rule and may not apply to rules set by different states and institutions.

Remove the deceased's name from the account. Add another person's name along with yours to give him/her authority to access the deposit box.

Always keep a current inventory of contents. It is advisable **not** to put an *original* trust, will, healthcare directive, or power of attorney in a safe deposit box. But it is a good idea to put a clearly marked *copy* of these documents. If the safe deposit box is owned by a sole individual, it will be sealed upon the owner's death. It may then take a court order to get the documents; this demonstrates why it is important to file original documents in a home safe or with your lawyer.

Safe Deposit Box, Home Safe

Provide appropriate information.

	Safe deposit box	Home safe
Location		
Where is the key?		
What is the combination number?		
If password, what is password?		
Who else has authority to access?		

Safe Deposit Box, Home Safe
Provide appropriate information.
(Continued)

Safe deposit box inventory	Home safe inventory

Taxes and Real Estate

Dealing with taxes and real estate can be one of the most complicated tasks after the death of a spouse. Entitlement to step-up taxes and federal and state tax adjustments are important to establish shortly after a death. Establish the fair market value (FMV) of all assets on the date of a spouse's death: car(s), house, investments, rentals, savings, individual stocks, mutual funds, etc. This will establish a cost basis for a step-up tax. Rules, requirements, and regulations vary depending on your state and other personal information. California is a community property state, which can affect almost every aspect of your property and taxes.

Hire a real estate appraiser to write a report on all residential property owned on the date of your spouse's death. "Comps" of similar properties, often done by real estate agents, are NOT acceptable cost basis by the IRS. When a surviving spouse sells residential property, the step-up tax basis is used.

The second consideration for a surviving spouse is the timing of the sale of residential property. A federal tax adjustment from the taxable profit is allowed for a surviving spouse who has lived in the primary residence for two of the past five years. If you sell your home within two years of a spouse's death, the tax adjustment is $500,000; if you sell later than two years, it is $250,000.

To establish a cost basis for step-up tax on taxable investments, such as stocks and mutual funds, call your stockbroker or investment company and request the price for each of your holdings on the date of your spouse's death.

You should also estimate the value of personal property, art, appliances, clothing, collections, computer, printer, scanner, electronics, furniture, gardening tools, house repair tools, jewelry, musical instruments, television, etc.

Expensive property, such as art, jewelry, and some electronics, may require certified appraisals.

Use the following worksheets to help keep track of the FMV for all your assets.

Benefits of Step-Up Basis and Income Tax Advantages of Sale of Personal Residence After Spouse's Death

Illustration of the advantage of selling a personal residence within two years of a spouse's death.

Initial purchase price of residence	$100,000
Date of death appraisal value: step-up adjusted cost value	$800,000
Surviving spouse sells house for	$1,300,000

Personal residence sold *within* 2 years from spouse's date of death

Selling price	$1,300,000
Less 6% real estate commission	-78,000
	$1,222,000
Less step-up adjusted cost, FMV at spouse's death	-800,000
Taxable Profit	$422,000
Less tax exclusion from profit	-500,000
Long-term gain, taxable profit	-0-

Personal residence sold 2 years *after* spouse's date of death

Selling price	$1,300,000
Less 6% real estate commission	-78,000
	$1,222,000
Less step-up adjusted cost, FMV at spouse's death	-800,000
Taxable Profit	$422,000
Less tax exclusion from profit	-250,000
Profit, long-term gain, taxable profit	$172,000

Fair Market Value (FMV) of Real Estate Assets

Keep all appraisals and pertinent information for future reference.

	Property address	Primary/ vacation/ rental	Lien holder	Loan balance	Tax information	Value on date of death
#1						
#2						
#3						
#4						
#5						

List Appraisal Values

	Name of appraisal company or name of appraiser	Personal residence	Rental property	Vacant land	Other property	Appraisal costs
#1		$	$	$	$	$
#2						
#3						
#4						
#5						

209

Fair Market Value (FMV) of Stocks, Mutual Funds, Other Investments

Do not include retirement accounts: Traditional IRA, Roth IRA, 401(k), or 403(b).

Name of stock/mutual fund		Broker of stock account	
Investment phone #		Account #	
# of shares		Purchase date	
Purchase price per share	Date of death price per share		Password

Name of stock/mutual fund		Broker of stock account	
Investment phone #		Account #	
# of shares		Purchase date	
Purchase price per share	Date of death price per share		Password

Name of stock/mutual fund		Broker of stock account	
Investment phone #		Account #	
# of shares		Purchase date	
Purchase price per share	Date of death price per share		Password

Name of stock/mutual fund		Broker of stock account	
Investment phone #		Account #	
# of shares		Purchase date	
Purchase price per share	Date of death price per share		Password

Fair Market Value (FMV) of Stocks, Mutual Funds, Other Investments
(Continued)

Name of stock/mutual fund	Broker of stock account
Investment phone #	Account #
# of shares	Purchase date

Purchase price per share	Date of death price per share	Password

Name of stock/mutual fund	Broker of stock account
Investment phone #	Account #
# of shares	Purchase date

Purchase price per share	Date of death price per share	Password

Name of stock/mutual fund	Broker of stock account
Investment phone #	Account #
# of shares	Purchase date

Purchase price per share	Date of death price per share	Password

Name of stock/mutual fund	Broker of stock account
Investment phone #	Account #
# of shares	Purchase date

Purchase price per share	Date of death price per share	Password

211

Fair Market Value (FMV) of Personal Property
Worksheet Example

Personal property	Appraised ✓	Estimated ✓	$ Value date of death
Computer: Apple iMac Desktop		✓	$2,500

Fair Market Value (FMV) of Personal Property

Personal property	Appraised ✓	Estimated ✓	$ Value date of death

Fair Market Value (FMV) of Personal Property
(Continued)

Personal property	Appraised ✓	Estimated ✓	$ Value date of death

Transportation

Establish the fair market value (FMV) for automobiles, mobile homes, RVs, boats, trailers, motorcycles, etc. Determine *Kelley Blue Book* values for all vehicles. Also remove the deceased's name from the DMV registration for each vehicle unless the vehicle is registered on an "and/or" basis. When the title is on an "and/or" basis, removing the deceased's name is not necessary, as either husband or wife can sign off on the title.

Notify all relevant insurance companies of the date of death and remove your spouse's name from all policies. Doing so may lower your premiums.

Fair Market Value (FMV) of Cars, Etc.

Name, make, model, year of vehicle	License number
Name(s) on title	Title location
Evaluation price date of death	Lease loan information
Odometer reading	Affidavit transfer w/out probate filed
Name, make, model, year of vehicle	License number
Name(s) on title	Title location
Evaluation price date of death	Lease loan information
Odometer reading	Affidavit transfer w/out probate filed
Name, make, model, year of vehicle	License number
Name(s) on title	Title location
Evaluation price date of death	Lease loan information
Odometer reading	Affidavit transfer w/out probate filed

Fair Market Value (FMV) of Cars, Etc.
(Continued)

Name, make, model, year of vehicle	License number
Name(s) on title	Title location
Evaluation price date of death	Lease loan information
Odometer reading	Affidavit transfer w/out probate filed
Name, make, model, year of vehicle	License number
Name(s) on title	Title location
Evaluation price date of death	Lease loan information
Odometer reading	Affidavit transfer w/out probate filed
Name, make, model, year of vehicle	License number
Name(s) on title	Title location
Evaluation price date of death	Lease loan information
Odometer reading	Affidavit transfer w/out probate filed
Name, make, model, year of vehicle	License number
Name(s) on title	Title location
Evaluation price date of death	Lease loan information
Odometer reading	Affidavit transfer w/out probate filed

Insurance Notifications

Name of company	Vehicle
Contact number	Website
PIN	Amount owed
Amount returned	Date deceased removed from policy
Name of company	Vehicle
Contact number	Website
PIN	Amount owed
Amount returned	Date deceased removed from policy
Name of company	Vehicle
Contact number	Website
PIN	Amount owed
Amount returned	Date deceased removed from policy
Name of company	Vehicle
Contact number	Website
PIN	Amount owed
Amount returned	Date deceased removed from policy

Insurance Notifications
(Continued)

Name of company	Vehicle
Contact number	Website
PIN	Amount owed
Amount returned	Date deceased removed from policy
Name of company	Vehicle
Contact number	Website
PIN	Amount owed
Amount returned	Date deceased removed from policy
Name of company	Vehicle
Contact number	Website
PIN	Amount owed
Amount returned	Date deceased removed from policy
Name of company	Vehicle
Contact number	Website
PIN	Amount owed
Amount returned	Date deceased removed from policy

AB Trust with Pour-Over Will

Review all wills, trusts, and directives regarding power of attorney for financial and health matters.

AB Trusts

A "bypass" trust is a living trust with an "AB" provision. AB living trusts were popular years ago. We had an AB trust but changed to a simple trust to avoid the extra work and required expertise. We included this information just so you would be aware of how an AB trust works. Talk to a professional when making decisions for your situation as regulations change in a blink of an eye.

When a spouse dies, assets will be divided evenly into the AB parts of the trust. File the deceased's original "pour-over will" with the Superior Court of California. Generally, it must be filed within ten days of death. Check with your county superior court for requirements. Keep a copy for your record.

If filing in the county of Ventura, send the deceased's original pour-over will by registered mail to: Attention: Probate Court, 4353 E. Vineyard Ave., Oxnard, CA 93009

The "B" portion of a trust becomes IRREVOCABLE on the date the first spouse dies. The surviving spouse is required by law to file federal and state tax returns each year on both portions of the trust until the estate is closed. He/she can use his/her own Social Security number for the "A" portion. For "B," use an Employer Identification Number (EIN) obtained for the deceased spouse.

Assets in Trusts A and B are interchangeable and can be interchanged any time, but you must keep documentation and Trust B must be funded to its original starting amount with certain allowances:

- Each year the surviving spouse can withdraw $5,000 or 5%, whichever is greater, of the B portion of the trust, which reduces the assets of the B portion of the trust must hold.
- If the B part of the trust gains in value, the new value is the amount B must keep funded.

Trust B is distributed to heirs upon death and closing of the surviving spouse's estate.

AB Trust
Divide Estate Assets

A simple example of how an AB Trust is divided.

Divide the estate assets in half. Place half the estate assets into A part of trust, surviving spouse. Place half the estate assets into B part of trust, deceased spouse. It does not matter which assets are placed in A or B. What matters is the VALUE. It must be an equal dollar amount. An easy way to remember who is A and who is B in an AB trust: A is the person **above ground**; B is the person **below ground**.

Dividing Estate Assets In Half
Calculation Example

Assets	FMV	A Trust surviving spouse	B Trust deceased spouse
House	$400,000		$400,000
Wife IRA	200,000	$200,000	
Husband IRA	200,000	200,000	
Stocks	80,000	40,000	40,000
CD/Cash	90,000	30,000	60,000
Other	30,000	30,000	
Totals	**$1,000,000**	**$500,000**	**$500,000**

Employer Identification Number (EIN)

EIN __ __ - __ __ __ __ __ __ __

An Employer Identification Number (EIN), a nine-digit taxpayer identification number issued by the IRS for the administration of tax laws, is used to identify the B portion of an AB trust. If an EIN is required for the deceased spouse for trust purposes, it can be obtained by the personal representative of the estate from the IRS. The EIN will identify the deceased's portion of the estate to the IRS when you file federal and state estate taxes.

To obtain an EIN, go to www.irs.gov. Enter "EIN" in the search field. A link to "Apply for an Employer Identification Number (EIN) Online" will become available. At this link you

will be able to complete an online application by filling out and submitting a request for Estate of Deceased Individual. Your application is validated during your online session. Once verified, an EIN is issued immediately. Obtaining an EIN is easiest online, but you can also receive an EIN from the IRS by phone or fax. **BE AWARE** of websites that charge you for the same form and services you can get for free from the IRS.

It is important that the EIN be kept in an accessible place. The deceased's EIN will be used instead of the deceased's Social Security number when filing estate taxes until the estate is closed. If the deceased person's estate has an AB trust, the representative of the estate is required by law to file Tax Form 1041 with the IRS on the deceased person's B portion of the trust to determine taxable gains on assets until the estate is closed.

CHAPTER 11

Closing an Estate

Closing an estate is complex. Professional help is necessary. The following story is an example of expenses incurred by a trustee closing an estate.

Following her parent's death, Ava, who had been named trustee of their estate, sought assistance from the lawyer responsible for preparing her parents trust. She quickly discovered that his charges were $350 an hour and that many questions she asked were answered by his secretary, who billed at $150 an hour. She also found billing charges were prorated minute to minute for services provided for partial hours. Ava was astonished to see that a monthly bill from the lawyer included several $20 charges for informational calls she made to the lawyer with questions that were quickly answered by his secretary.

Roy, my husband, helped Ava change to a lawyer whose charges were more equitable. Roy and Ava then tackled the grunt work of gathering the information the current lawyer needed. Filling out the worksheets and evaluating the guidance in this workbook helped.

Throughout this workbook, including this chapter, we have provided worksheets for you to complete, starting simply and working up to the grand finale—Closing the Estate. You will find that many of the forms you need to fill out, debts you need to pay, distributions of assets to beneficiaries, etc., need the same information that you now have at your fingertips. This will be a time-saver and a tension reliever. You will now be able to limit the work that must be done by a lawyer. Yay! However, laws and regulations change quickly and vary from state to state, so it is always in your best interest to at least keep an estate and/or tax attorney in the loop.

Social Security, Medicare Notification

Notify Social Security as soon as possible when family member dies. In most cases, the funeral director will report the person's death to Social Security. Give the funeral director the deceased's Social Security number so he/she can report the death.

Fill in all applicable information.

Deceased name   Social Security #

Date of death

Surviving spouse name   Social Security #

Social Security representative name

Social Security representative ID/title

Date of conversation

Notes

Deceased Personal Information
Fill in all applicable information.

Full legal name

Maiden name

Nickname

Phone #

Street address,
city, state, zip

Date of birth

Date of death

Death location

Social Security #

Birthplace (city, state)

Marriage date

Divorce date

Father of deceased name

Father's date of birth

Father's birthplace

Father's date of death, if applicable

Father's location of death, if applicable

Mother of deceased name

Mother's maiden name

Mother's date of birth

Mother's birthplace

Mother's date of death, if applicable

Mother's location of death, if applicable

Child/Children of Deceased

Name of Deceased

Child's name	Date of birth	Gender

Address, street, city, state, zip

Home phone	Cell phone	Email

Child's name	Date of birth	Gender

Address, street, city, state, zip

Home phone	Cell phone	Email

Child's name	Date of birth	Gender

Address, street, city, state, zip

Home phone	Cell phone	Email

Child's name	Date of birth	Gender

Address, street, city, state, zip

Home phone	Cell phone	Email

Child's name	Date of birth	Gender

Address, street, city, state, zip

Home phone	Cell phone	Email

Child/Children of Deceased
(Continued)

Name of Deceased

Child's name	Date of birth	Gender

Address, street, city, state, zip

Home phone	Cell phone	Email

Child's name	Date of birth	Gender

Address, street, city, state, zip

Home phone	Cell phone	Email

Child's name	Date of birth	Gender

Address, street, city, state, zip

Home phone	Cell phone	Email

Child's name	Date of birth	Gender

Address, street, city, state, zip

Home phone	Cell phone	Email

Child's name	Date of birth	Gender

Address, street, city, state, zip

Home phone	Cell phone	Email

Stepchildren of Deceased

Name of Deceased

Child's name	Date of birth	Gender

Address, street, city, state, zip

Home phone	Cell phone	Email

Child's name	Date of birth	Gender

Address, street, city, state, zip

Home phone	Cell phone	Email

Child's name	Date of birth	Gender

Address, street, city, state, zip

Home phone	Cell phone	Email

Child's name	Date of birth	Gender

Address, street, city, state, zip

Home phone	Cell phone	Email

Child's name	Date of birth	Gender

Address, street, city, state, zip

Home phone	Cell phone	Email

Stepchildren of Deceased
(Continued)

Name of Deceased

Child's name	Date of birth	Gender

Address, street, city, state, zip

Home phone	Cell phone	Email

Child's name	Date of birth	Gender

Address, street, city, state, zip

Home phone	Cell phone	Email

Child's name	Date of birth	Gender

Address, street, city, state, zip

Home phone	Cell phone	Email

Child's name	Date of birth	Gender

Address, street, city, state, zip

Home phone	Cell phone	Email

Child's name	Date of birth	Gender

Address, street, city, state, zip

Home phone	Cell phone	Email

Grandchildren of Deceased

Name of Deceased

Child's name	Date of birth	Gender

Address, street, city, state, zip

Home phone	Cell phone	Email

Child's name	Date of birth	Gender

Address, street, city, state, zip

Home phone	Cell phone	Email

Child's name	Date of birth	Gender

Address, street, city, state, zip

Home phone	Cell phone	Email

Child's name	Date of birth	Gender

Address, street, city, state, zip

Home phone	Cell phone	Email

Child's name	Date of birth	Gender

Address, street, city, state, zip

Home phone	Cell phone	Email

Grandchildren of Deceased
(Continued)

Name of Deceased

Child's name	Date of birth	Gender

Address, street, city, state, zip

Home phone	Cell phone	Email

Child's name	Date of birth	Gender

Address, street, city, state, zip

Home phone	Cell phone	Email

Child's name	Date of birth	Gender

Address, street, city, state, zip

Home phone	Cell phone	Email

Child's name	Date of birth	Gender

Address, street, city, state, zip

Home phone	Cell phone	Email

Child's name	Date of birth	Gender

Address, street, city, state, zip

Home phone	Cell phone	Email

Great-grandchildren of Deceased

Name of Deceased

Child's name		Date of birth	Gender

Address, street, city, state, zip

Home phone	Cell phone	Email	

Child's name		Date of birth	Gender

Address, street, city, state, zip

Home phone	Cell phone	Email	

Child's name		Date of birth	Gender

Address, street, city, state, zip

Home phone	Cell phone	Email	

Child's name		Date of birth	Gender

Address, street, city, state, zip

Home phone	Cell phone	Email	

Child's name		Date of birth	Gender

Address, street, city, state, zip

Home phone	Cell phone	Email	

Great-grandchildren of Deceased
(Continued)

Name of Deceased

Child's name	Date of birth	Gender

Address, street, city, state, zip

Home phone	Cell phone	Email

Child's name	Date of birth	Gender

Address, street, city, state, zip

Home phone	Cell phone	Email

Child's name	Date of birth	Gender

Address, street, city, state, zip

Home phone	Cell phone	Email

Child's name	Date of birth	Gender

Address, street, city, state, zip

Home phone	Cell phone	Email

Child's name	Date of birth	Gender

Address, street, city, state, zip

Home phone	Cell phone	Email

Heir(s) and Beneficiaries of Deceased

Name of Deceased

Name	Social Security #

Birth date	Relationship: son, daughter, husband, wife, friend	

Address, street, city, state, zip

Home phone	Cell phone	Email
Selected benefit	Money distributed	Distribution date

Name	Social Security #

Birth date	Relationship: son, daughter, husband, wife, friend	

Address, street, city, state, zip

Home phone	Cell phone	Email
Selected benefit	Money distributed	Distribution date

Name	Social Security #

Birth date	Relationship: son, daughter, husband, wife, friend	

Address, street, city, state, zip

Home phone	Cell phone	Email
Selected benefit	Money distributed	Distribution date

Heir(s) and Beneficiaries of Deceased
(Continued)

Name of Deceased

Name		Social Security #
Birth date	Relationship: son, daughter, husband, wife, friend	

Address, street, city, state, zip

Home phone	Cell phone	Email
Selected benefit	Money distributed	Distribution date

Name		Social Security #
Birth date	Relationship: son, daughter, husband, wife, friend	

Address, street, city, state, zip

Home phone	Cell phone	Email
Selected benefit	Money distributed	Distribution date

Name		Social Security #
Birth date	Relationship: son, daughter, husband, wife, friend	

Address, street, city, state, zip

Home phone	Cell phone	Email
Selected benefit	Money distributed	Distribution date

California Requirements

Each state has its own set of rules for closing an estate. In California, you are allowed to avoid probate by using a small estate affidavit to close an estate meeting the following criteria: worth less than $166,250 at date of death, does not include real property, and forty days have passed since the deceased's death.

Legal definition of:

- personal property is **movable**; belongings exclusive of land and buildings.
- real property is **immovable** property—it's land and anything attached to the land.

Non-Trust Assets

Sometimes an individual creates a trust but neglects to add some or all of his/her assets into the trust. Also, purchases may have been made after the trust was created and those assets not added. Probate may be required for the unadded assets depending on total value. Without the transfer of assets into a trust, the trust is a useless piece of paper.

If your trust doesn't have a pour-over will, property left out of the trust passes to your heirs by intestate succession—the closest kin who can inherit from you in the absence of a will under state law. This complication can be avoided by creating a pour-over will when creating and funding your trust. A pour-over directs assets that were not funded (assets not added to a trust) now to be included. Be aware that a pour-over will is still a will, and in some cases needs to be probated.

General Probate Process

Probate rules and proceedings vary from state to state. A probate court determines who will be the executor, executrix, or administrator of an estate and guardian of minor children. The court approves the final distribution of the estate's assets.

In California, the probate process can take one to two years and can be expensive—generally 2% to 5% of gross estate value. The court decides the probate method to be used to process the estate. Small estate administration involves estates with small dollar value and less formalities.

- Probate can be fully court-supervised for all or part of the process.
- Probate can be unsupervised or include little supervision, with some reporting requirements.
- To start or open probate, an estate personal representative must submit the original will.
- If the deceased had no will, the court appoints an administrator of the estate.

- When applicable, a trustee of a trust must submit an original pour-over will to the probate court.
- Once the court approves the personal representative of an estate, the probate registrar will issue a "letter of administration" or "letters testamentary." The holder of the letter has the authority to perform duties to close the estate.

For easy reference, listed are the types of estate and representatives who close the estate.

NO WILL (INTESTATE), PROBATE
Administrator of Estate

....

The administrator of the estate must have a letter of authority from the probate court to conduct business on behalf of the estate.

WILL, PROBATE
Executor (male) of Estate or Executrix (female) of Estate

....

The executor or executrix of the estate must have a letter of authority from the probate court to conduct business on behalf of the estate.
Estates valued under $166,250 may be able to avoid probate court proceedings.

TRUST
Trustee of Trust Estate

....

No probate court approval needed.

POUR-OVER WILL INCLUDED WITH A TRUST
Trustee of Trust Estate

If pour-over will value is more than $166,250, probate is required.

Mary—P Word

Mary, who had been widowed for forty-seven years, lived in Newbury Park in a double-wide mobile home she had purchased with her late husband.

Mary took care of all her finances. Raised in the Depression, she knew how to stretch a dollar and would take her savings from bank to bank to get the highest bank and CD rate. She lived only on Social Security after her husband's death and had no pension, 401(k), IRA, or inheritance money to fall back on. When she shopped for groceries, she would head straight to the bargains in the back. She purchased day-old bread, which made the best bread pudding ever.

When she died at the age of ninety, her family was surprised to realize her estate was worth $500,000. Yep! That's no typing error. $500,000. Mary had managed to put away $465,000 in savings and certificates of deposit, and her beloved 1958 double-wide trailer sold for $35,000. Mary's will left her estate to her two sons.

Normally a $500,000 estate with no protection from a trust would have to go through that dreaded *P* word, probate. But the law has many twists and turns, and good fortune graced Mary's estate. It turned out Mary's $500,000 estate didn't have to be probated. Why? A mobile home in California, if parked on rented land such as a mobile home community, is not considered real estate property but personal property. Mary's estate was able to use the *affidavit for transfer of personal property* form when selling her mobile home, because it was classified as personal, not real estate, property. The same affidavit is used when selling automobiles and boats.

Mary's accounts were held jointly in her name and the names of her two sons. All three were equal holders. At her death, Mary's sons removed her name from each account. This removed the accounts from her estate. The estate value was no longer $500,000 but $35,000, the amount earned from the sale of the trailer. No probate required.

Probate was avoided in this case, but adding each son as a joint owner of her bank accounts could have been catastrophic. If one of her sons had been sued, the court could have attached one or all accounts. And either son, before or after Mary's death, had the legal right to withdraw all the money and close the accounts. A better way of sharing her estate with her sons would have been to have added each son as a beneficiary to each banking account. At her passing, the money would have gone directly to them, also avoiding estate probate. The money would not have been subjected to a lawsuit that the sons might have incurred while Mary was still living.

Closing an Estate

The following pages list some of the steps to guide you in closing an estate. Some items are applicable to probated estates, some to trusts, and some to both. Refer back to Chapter 10 for more in-depth discussions, worksheets, and charts related to many of these tasks and information regarding taxes and insurance.

Estate Closing Tasks

Make an appointment with the individual who set up the trust or will.

Name of deceased

Lawyer of will or trust   Phone

Address

Appointment date   Appointment time

If the deceased had real property, you are required to notify the county assessor office within 150 days of the date of death, or if the estate is probated, you can notify the county assessor office at the same time the estate inventory and appraisal is filed.

County Assessor Office

Name of county assessor office

Assessor office telephone number

Forms needed

Date assessor office notified

Estate's Responsibilities to
Probate Court Checklist

✓

	File a death certificate with the court.
	File the original will for probate. Prove the will's validity by providing statements from one or more witnesses to the will.
	If there is no will, submit an intestacy form with the court.
	Obtain a letter of authority from the probate court, in the county where the deceased person was living at the time of death, to conduct business on behalf of the estate.
	Post bond if required. The amount of bond depends on the size of the estate.
	Appoint guardians for minor children, if required.
	File a detailed inventory and valuation of the estate within one to six months of death.

File Birth, Death, and Marriage Certificates Checklist

✓

	Request twelve to fifteen certified death certificates from the funeral home.
	Make extra copies of birth, death, and marriage certificates, as insurance companies and other organizations may require them.

Review Wills/Trusts/Power of Attorney for Financial and Health Checklist

✓

	Review each for any special distributions or requests.

Social Security, Medicare, Medi-Cal Notification Checklist

✓

	Call Social Security, 800-772-1213, to inform them of deceased's passing and date of death. If applicable, SSA will report the information to Medicare and Medicaid (in California, Medi-Cal).

Open a Checking Account in "Name of the Estate" Checklist

✓

	Use this account for all transactions involving the estate, ensuring estate assets are separate from your own personal accounts.

✓	**Set Up "Estate Receivables Log" and "Estate Expenses Log" Checklist**
	The personal representative of an estate has a fiduciary duty to account for all estate funds. For probate, logs are required to be presented to the court. For a trust, distributions are accountable to the heirs of the trust.

✓	**Miscellaneous Personal Representative of a Probated Estate Responsibilities Checklist**
	List special distributions from the will. Discuss with heirs.
	Mail notices to creditors.
	Locate and review all financial records: tax returns, stocks, bonds, etc.
	Arrange for upkeep and maintenance of all real estate properties.
	Identify all non-probated property items that the estate will distribute, such as beneficiary inheritance items.
	Notify all interested persons, beneficiaries, and heirs that the estate is in probate process. File proof that you properly mailed notices.
	When appropriate, distribute funds for accounts that are owed to estate beneficiaries. This will reduce the estate's value.
	Publish a public notice in local newspapers according to court rules.
	File with the court a list of approved or denied creditor claims.
	Pay all funeral expenses.
	File for all Social Security, civil service, and veteran's benefits.
	Check with the court for claims filed against the estate.
	If applicable, arrange for sale of estate property and assets.

Establish Fair Market Value (FMV) for All Assets Checklist

✓	
	Establish FMVs for all assets on date of death: car(s), house, investments, rentals, savings, individual stocks, mutual funds, etc. FMV establishes a new cost basis for step-up tax basis for beneficiaries and heirs.
	Hire a real estate appraiser to write a report on all real estate property owned on date of death.
	Use step-up tax basis for a new cost basis for selling assets.
	California doesn't have an estate or inheritance tax. Your estate is allowed FMV of all assets up to $5.3 million before requiring federal estate tax. Consult a tax accountant.
	Refer to Chapter 10 for more information about FMVs and step-up tax basis. Worksheets and guidelines have been included to help with stated tasks.

Handle Vehicle Assets Checklist

✓	
	Get *Kelley Blue Book* values for all vehicles.
	File an *Affidavit for Transfer Without Probate* to transfer items in this category out of the estate to prevent them from being included as a probate asset.
	Notify insurance companies of the owner's death. Establish a contact person and ask about continuation of the policy/policies until vehicle(s) are sold. Remove deceased's name from policies.
	If necessary, pay off vehicle loans.

Pay Federal and State Estate Taxes Checklist

✓	
	File Federal Form 1041 with the IRS for each year the estate is open. Use EIN in place of Social Security number on tax returns, if applicable. (See Chapter 10 for more information on EINs.)
	File state tax returns for property in other states, if applicable.
	Pay or deposit any proceeds to deceased estate checking account.

✓	Make Arrangements for Life Insurance, Annuity Policies Checklist
	Contact all insurance policyholders for information regarding the beneficiary/beneficiaries and payout amount(s).
	Notify beneficiary/beneficiaries about how to claim their benefit(s).
	If there are no beneficiaries, notify each insurance plan of deceased's death and arrange to cash out.
	If you are the executor of an estate, you may be required to file IRS Forms 712 (Life Insurance Statement) and 706 (United States Estate and Generation-Skipping Transfer) with the estate tax return. Beneficiaries receiving life insurance benefits are not taxed.
	Deposit cash-out proceeds in "Deceased Estate" checking account.
	Browse through the deceased's checkbook register or canceled checks to see if any checks were paid to an insurance company. Check with the deceased's banks and credit unions for any accidental death $1,000 policies.

✓	Cash Deposits/Checking/Savings/Credit Union/Other Checklist
	Delay closing accounts until all automatic deposits and auto-pays are resolved.
	Pay off balances.
	Total collected balances of accounts and add to the estate checking account.

✓	Medical, Drug, Dental, Vision Insurance Plan(s) Checklist
	Notify each insurance plan of death.
	Pay all balances owed from deceased estate checking account.
	Collect all refunds or double payments deceased may have paid to insurance companies. Deposit in deceased estate checking account.

Hospital, Other Healthcare Facilities, Providers Checklist

✓	
	Contact all healthcare providers and pay any balances owed. Request all refunds entitled to estate.
	File necessary insurance claims.

Employee Wages, Pension(s) Checklist

✓	
	Notify the deceased employer's human resources office of death. Apply for any unpaid salary and employee benefits: life insurance, etc.
	Collect any unpaid wages due to the deceased.
	Deposit all pension funds owed to the deceased in estate checking account.
	Determine if a family member is entitled to continue or receive the deceased's pension.

Debit/Credit Cards Checklist

✓	
	Notify debit/credit card companies of death. Note that a financial institution will immediately cancel a credit or debit card when notified of account holder's death.
	Check if any automatic payments are in progress. If necessary, change auto-pay arrangements to an authorized card.
	Pay off balances.
	Cancel credit/debit card accounts.
	Add or subtract money accrued from these accounts to estate accounts.

Loans, Credit Bureaus Checklist

✓	
	Notify each creditor of death and request billing invoice if money is owed.
	If possible, pay off loan balances using deceased estate checking account.
	Retain billing invoices.
	Retain "Account Paid in Full" receipts.
	Report the death in writing to Equifax, Experian, and TransUnion credit bureaus. Request the agencies deny issuing credit in deceased's name. Include your information: name, contact information, and relationship to the deceased. Include deceased's information: deceased's name, Social Security number, last address, date of birth, and date of death, and a copy of the death certificate.
	Add or subtract money accrued in accounts. Post to estate accounts.

Empty Safe Deposit Box and Home Safe Checklist

✓	
	Access the safe deposit box with a court order or with a person who has the authority to open it. Inventory and remove the contents. Disburse as appropriate.
	Close the account.
	Inventory the home safe. Disburse as appropriate.

Cancel Subscriptions, Memberships Checklist

✓	
	Cancel subscriptions to newspapers, magazines, health clubs, etc.
	Ask for a partial refund on unused portions of subscriptions and memberships. Add refunds to estate checking account.

Review Auto-Pay Bills Checklist

✓	
	Review bills being paid automatically out of estate checking or savings accounts or credit accounts.
	After reviewing bills, cancel those not necessary to run the household or estate.

✓	**Close Rental Property Checklist**
	Notify landlord of deceased's death. Show death certificate.
	Determine if deceased had a lease and what obligations need to be met.
	Establish move-out date and pay any rent due from estate checking account.
	Determine what obligations need to be met for return of security deposit.
	Arrange to have rental cleaned and repairs made.
	Maintain an inventory and acquire FMV of each item in home. Distribute to beneficiaries, sell, donate, or dispose of personal items. Deposit proceeds in estate checking account.
	Return all rented or leased equipment or electronics, such as television cable box.
	Notify and cancel utilities. Pay any balances. Collect any refunds.
	Secure rental deposit from landlord and deposit in estate checking account.
	Cancel renter's insurance policies, if applicable. Ask for refund for unused portion of policy.

Rental Worksheet

Fill in all available information.

Revenue from property sold, security deposit, etc.	Date	Estate checking account deposit

Liabilities paid out	Date	Withdrawals

✓	**Maintain Financial Records Checklist**
	Record all income from insurance companies: CDs, cash, money, money market, savings, checking, and all other investment accounts.
	Pay or deposit any proceeds to deceased estate checking account.
	Record all proceeds from property sale(s).
	Record all expenses closing the estate.

✓	**Close Utilities, Trash Collection, Etc. Checklist**
	Remove deceased's name where applicable.
	Pay all account balances owed from estate checking account.
	Continue utilities and trash collections until appropriate to cancel.
	Stop continued auto-payments.
	Close accounts.

✓	**Notify Post Office, Homeowner's Association Checklist**
	Notify post office of deceased's death and forward mail to executor, administrator, or trustee's address. In order for the post office to forward deceased's mail, they require a death certificate and proof you are responsible for the estate.
	Notify homeowner's association of death. Continue homeowner's association payment until appropriate to cancel.

✓	**Notify Beneficiaries Checklist**
	By registered letter, notify IRA, 401(k), and 403(b) beneficiaries.
	Advise beneficiaries to contact their financial advisor for help in transferring these accounts. See more information in Chapters 6 and 10 regarding these accounts.

✓	**Distribute Assets Checklist**
	Collect money and pay bills that are the estate's responsibility.
	Determine net worth of estate for distributing to heirs.
	Per probate rules, petition court for personal representative and attorney fees.
	Per probate rules, after all the money is collected and bills paid, receive court's permission to distribute assets to heirs.
	Distribute all probate-court-approved assets.
	Trust estates distributes all assets; no approval from court is needed. Obtain receipt for each asset.
	Present a *Final Accounting* report to the probate court to close the estate and show that all debts and taxes have been paid and all property and assets have been distributed.
	Present a *Final Accounting* letter to beneficiaries of the trust.

✓	**Estate Closing Checklist**
	For probate, file all remaining required documents with the court.
	Close the estate.
	For probated estates, obtain court approval to discharge the estate's personal representative.
	Keep all records for at least one year.

Closing Alice's Estate—F Word

Alice, a sweet lady in her eighties, had no known living relative or any close friends. The bad news: She was frail and showing signs of dementia. The good news: She was a cancer survivor, lucky enough to own her home debt-free, and had considerable savings.

Steve, recently divorced, was living in Tucson and wandering about town looking for a new enterprise. As president and owner of Acme Wrecking Company, he looked reputable on first impression. Business was good, but his purchase of a $65,000 used dump truck in need of new tires increased his indebtedness. Then he met Alice.

Alice had hired Steve to do work on her property. Soon Steve was living in her home, parking construction equipment, and stockpiling salvaged materials on her large plot of land. Perfect match. Steve needed a room. Alice needed a caretaker and handyman.

Meanwhile, Human Services, aware of Alice's circumstances, had started court proceedings requesting fiduciary responsibility for her care and finances. But Steve, never missing an opportunity, informed them that he and Alice had married two days earlier in Las Vegas. As her legal husband, he now controlled Alice's care—and finances.

Alice was eighty-six, and Steve was sixty-one and now set for life. He had a place to live and park his equipment, and money in the bank. What could go wrong?

Boom! A couple of years later, Alice wandered into the kitchen. She found Steve lying on the floor. Paramedics said he had died from a heart attack. Wow! Talk about unexpected.

After Steve's death, the state successfully received a court order to take over the *fiduciary duties* (the *F word*) of Alice's estate and oversee her care. Alice was placed in a nursing facility; a bank was appointed to sell her home and pay her bills. $$$$ quickly flew out of the estate into court funds and bank assets. Alice lived less than a year after Steve's death, and incomprehensibly, all her money and assets were depleted by the close of her estate. In a twist of fate, Alice, 88, died on the same day and month as Steve's birth.

Conclusion

Little did we know when we started writing this publication how relevant our insights would be to people's lives. Our book encourages people to prepare for changes and emergencies. Our goal was to establish a pathway and provide worksheets to guide you to secure the hidden treasures of your life to share with your loved ones. We are so blessed and happy we could include personal stories and our experiences. Completion of our workbook is a gift of love to yourself and your family. Thank you for participating in this journey with us to improve your life in this way! Hurray for YOU!

Acknowledgments

We sincerely believe the truism, "It takes a village."

This is so true in book publishing. We are so thankful for the talent,

support, and honesty of all the people we have met in our endeavor,

especially the Awesome Foursome: Marla, Tammy, Kelly, and Wyn.

We have had such a wonderful learning experience,

and we hope our book provides this to you also.

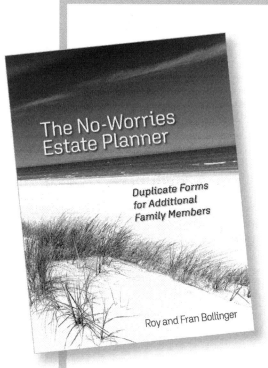

Your whole family benefits from estate planning.

To make it easier for family participation and sharing, you can purchase our **No Worries Estate Planner: Duplicate Forms for Additional Family Members**, a packet of convenient duplicate forms used in our book.

Available on Amazon and other online booksellers.

INDEX

Forms are indicated by numbers in italic type, e.g., 14-15. Non-italicized numbers indicate textual discussion of topic. Numbers, e.g., 401(k), will be indexed as if spelled out.

Made in the USA
Middletown, DE
13 May 2021